TO GOD I GIVE MY MELODY

To God I Give My Melody

Reflections for Worship

SUSAN PALO CHERWIEN

MorningStar Music Publishers, Inc.
1727 Larkin Williams Road, Saint Louis, Missouri 63026-2024
morningstarmusic.com

Printed in the United States of America

ISBN 978-0-944529-79-9

Library of Congress Control Number: 2019939869

To David
whose music and imagination
give the printed words life
give the printed notes song

CONTENTS

PRELUDE

Singing together in community is a powerful, life-shaping activity. The deep breathing required massages our inner bodies and quiets the brain. The resonance causes us to vibrate together, forming a community out of diverse people. And when we are singing holy stories together, holy thoughts together, we are lifted into a different way of seeing and being.

Over my entire lifetime, I have been surrounded by the hymns of the church, and for the last almost 40 years, I have participated in hymn festivals, mostly in partnership with my spouse David Cherwien. When we first began, I would pull just about every book of theology, poetry, spirituality, and devotions off the shelves, and there I would sit with these piles of books around me, trying to find the exactly perfect reading to help lead us into the singing of the hymn to come. Noticing my frustration at not finding *The Perfect Reading*, David finally suggested that maybe I should try writing the reflections myself. This is the third volume of those reflections, so kindly made available to others by Mark Lawson at MorningStar Music Publishers.

Well-known hymns can become like paintings hung in the same place for a long time—we walk past them and don't notice them anymore. We name them, we know them, we know what they mean, and that's the end of our thought. And so what I try to do in these reflections, on behalf of all of us, is to look at these marvelous texts with new eyes, with beginner's mind, asking myself, "what have I not seen before?" Or, if I have been reading Hildegard von Bingen's visions, for example, "what seems different in this hymn in light of Hildegard?" So, I hope to offer a new door into the hymn, a somewhat different vista. It is my hope that I have sometimes succeeded.

There are no original thoughts in these pages—someone else's sermon, someone else's scientific treatise, the newspaper, the Bible, conversations, books, books, books, paintings, poetry, and the natural world all weave together in these reflections. I hope you will forgive me a few repeated favorite stories, a few repeated favorite quotes. I hope you will forgive me if you had the idea first, and I no longer remember where I heard it or saw it. We are all on this pilgrimage together, and I am grateful to all the thinkers and dreamers and riskers whose writing or speech or art over the centuries has shaped the words I have woven together here.

"To God I give my melody
And thanks for all eternity."

Martin Luther, "A Preface for All Good Hymnals," 1538

—Susan Palo Cherwien

TE DEUM LAUDAMUS
LET US PRAISE GOD

I. Theology and Song

You Are God.

All our worship
begins and ends with God.
All our praise
begins and ends with God.
Our liturgy begins
"The grace of God..."
and our liturgy ends
"Thanks be to God!"
"You Are God"
is the beginning of all our thought
it is the beginning
of all our questions
it is the ultimate answer we seek.
The holy writings teach us
that God spoke the universe into being.
God said...
God sent out sound—
vibration—
And the now-universe responded
by vibrating
with the Voice of God.
Everything that exists
is in vibration
and all vibrating bodies
affect all other vibrating bodies
earth vibrates at roughly 8 cycles per second
the Sun sends out sound waves
from its erupting surface
black holes in other galaxies
sing out their unique keys—
B-flats and D-flats and A-flats—

And vibrating with the
Voice of God,
we sing out.

The first three bones
to be completely formed in the human fetus
are the three small bones
in the middle ear.
We are made to be hearing creatures—
hearing God's Voice—
hearing the universe's song
hearing each other.

The nerve from the eardrum
branches
and ends in the tongue.
We are made to be singing creatures—
vibrating with the Voice of God
singing praise.

You are God—
sending out song,
creating the universe.
St. Gregory of Nyssa writes:
"The whole cosmos
is a kind of musical harmony
whose musician
is God."
Hymnist Martin Franzmann adds his voice:
"Theology is doxology.
Theology must sing."

You are God.
We praise You.

II. The Word and Song

In the beginning
was the Word—
the creative power of God—
and the Word became flesh
and dwelt among us,
Worthy of all worship.

Singing from the thirteenth century
Adam Scotus describes the Word as
"instilling sweet sound
in the faithful"
by bringing together
the perfect fourth
of the four cardinal virtues
with the perfect fifth
of the five senses,
creating
"the sweet melody
of the perfect Octave."
Christ,
the Perfect Octave,
balancing
Flesh and Spirit
Human and Divine
Sense and Virtue
Earth and Heaven
brought together in perfection
in the Word.
In the musical harmony

of the cosmos,
Christ is the perfect Octave
vibrating perfectly
with both
the divine and the human
to bring us into like vibration.
The Word—
worthy of all worship.

The great hymnist St. Ephrem the Syrian sings to us:
"[Christ] clothed himself in language
so that he might clothe us in his mode of life."
Alleluia.

III. Community and Song

From the fourth century,
St. Augustine joins in the singing.
In an Easter sermon he writes:
"You have heard the words
Sing to the LORD a new song.
You want to know what is God's glory?
God's glory is the assembly of saints.
The glory of the one who is sung about
is nothing other than the one
who sings about it.
Become yourself the glory that you sing of."

When we sing hymns to God together
when we sing praise together
when we worship God together
we are being formed
into a glorious body—
a glorious "We."
From the twentieth century
composer Nadia Boulanger adds,
"The music of the church
makes one forget self.
It is ridiculous to use
the pronoun "I"
in Chartres Cathedral."
For Hildegard von Bingen,
we become part of the
"cosmic symphony."
The universe vibrates with the
voice of God
the perfect Octave of the Word,
the Christ,
beckons us into like harmony

and the Spirit urges us
to become the glory we sing of.
All our worship begins and ends
with God.

Paul Westermeyer
adds his voice to this celestial harmony:
"Hymn singing is . . . delightful play
just like all music-making.
But it is not a mindless
or entertaining diversion
that gives the church a break
from the really important stuff
or serves as a manipulatively
attractive ploy.
It is the sounding form
of the Body of Christ . . .
The church's song is as important
as all the other things
to which the church is called . . ."

All our worship begins and ends
with God
God most excellent
God most beautiful
God most loving
God most true.

You are God, we sing,
we praise You.

WORSHIP IN SONG: JOY, HOPE, PEACE

I. **Joy**

II. **Hope**

III. **Peace**

I. Joy

In deep space there is a fossil
And that fossil
is a sound
We cannot hear it
We cannot touch it
We can only see it
And what we see
are pressure waves
pressure waves from the past
passing between us and the light of distant stars—
the waves of a fossil sound:
the music of
the Big Bang—
a descending
glissando
moving from high pitches
into deep rumbling bass tones
as the universe expanded.
And from its first moments
the music of the universe
established its overtones
the same sequence
of overtones
that our voices
produce when we sing
the same overtones
that orchestras create
with string
and metal and wood

that whales sing
that black holes chant
and starsong
and birdsong
and cricketsong
all resonating
all resounding
with the innate harmonics
of the universe—
a choir of being
a choir of existence
a choir of "I Am"
and "We Are"
a creation choir
of pure joy

Prayer *(after "Joy"):*

Blessed are you, O God,
for your most Beautiful Voice
set the creation
in motion;
May our songs
set in motion the joy and wonder
that reside in every heart.
Amen

II. Hope

Everything that exists
is in vibration
And every vibrating body
affects and changes
other vibrating bodies.
Bernice Johnson Reagon said:
"Songs are a way
to get to singing.
The singing is what
you're aiming for.
You cannot sing a song
and not change
your condition."
Singing,
we breathe together
we vibrate together
we become together
and if we are singing beauty together
we become more beautiful together
and the universe receives
and resonates with the beauty we are singing
and becomes more beautiful.
And if we are singing love together
we become more loving together
and the universe receives
and resonates with the love we are singing
and becomes more loving.

And if we are singing hope together
we become more hopeful
and the universe receives...
and becomes...
And if we sing mercy together...
And if we sing compassion...
And if we sing...

Prayer *(after "Hope"):*

Blessed are you, O God,
for your Loving Song
continues to create the world;
May our hearts always be open
to the deep Becoming that is life.
Amen

III. Peace

The universe is becoming
Just as we are becoming
And the movement
of the universe
is toward diversity—
ever new stars
ever new planets
ever new plants
ever new animals
ever new people—
all sparkling harmonics
of the One Foundational Tone
all overtones
of a sounding
pedal tone
The Source of All—
underlying all creation—
a Source that creates
and loves diversity
delights in myriad forms
moves toward complexity
all notes
all overtones
all voices
emanating from
sounding from
this one Loving Sound
creating the choir
of the universe
the song of existence

each voice unique
each voice precious
connected to every other
unique and precious voice
beautiful
beloved
all harmonics
rising from the One Beautiful Music
underlying all
that is.

Prayer *(after "Peace"):*

Blessed are you, O God,
for everything that you have made
is your Beloved:
May our lives be radiant
with the Loving Music
that you have sung
into all things.
Amen

A THOUSAND VOICES SING PRAISE

I. Even the Sun Has a Song

II. Songs of Our Ancestors

III. Letting Go

IV. Songs of Peace

I. Even the Sun Has a Song

Even the sun
has a song to sing

Astrophysicists
observing the sun
at the
Goddard Space Center
Noticed ripples
And fluctuations
On the surface of earth's star.
They adjusted instruments
Fine-tuned calibrations
Trying to eliminate the movement.
Until they realized
That the ripples they were seeing
Were sound waves
What they were seeing
Was the song of the sun.
The sun was singing
The surface of the sun
Is vibrating with
10,000 frequencies—
low tones out of the depths
of the sun
high tones from nearer
the surface
of the sun.

The same furnace
That is flaming forth light
Is sending out song
Burning and bursting
And sending out song
Like a choir of angels
Like a night sky full of light
Perhaps
If the time is right
Perhaps
If we have ears to hear
We will not only
Feel the sun's light
On our faces
But we will also
Someday
Hear the sunlight
carrying the song
of our nearest star:
Gloria

II Songs of Our Ancestors

Our spirals of DNA
Carry within them
Not only the seeds of our ancestors—
Their physical characteristics
Blue eyes
Black curly hair
A proclivity to knee injury—
Our DNA also
Carries within us
The songs
Of our ancestors
Their wishes
their aspirations
Their holy dreams
Our DNA carries the vibration
Of their sacred stories
The music of the bone flutes
They played in dark caves
Their images of the Divine
Their deepest loves
Their reaching after stars
Their hymns
their psalms
vibrate within us
singing with us
cheering us on

And when we
open ourselves
to the Divine—
when the Divine
comes together
with human DNA—
new creation
new vibration
new song.

III. Letting Go

Not all that is planted in us
by our ancestors
should be treasured
and clung to
not all that is planted
bears good fruit
hatreds feuds walls
misunderstanding separation
flawed belief
fear
there is chaff
mixed in with the grain
chaff that must
be
sifted out
consciously   carefully
old hurts
wounds
wars
vibrate across the centuries
through us
and take form
in this time
in this place

unless we
take the sickle
in hand
consciously   carefully
and harvest
and sift
and choose
which songs we will
sing
and
sing on.

IV. Songs of Peace

It is at the
Core of the sun
(Thou burning sun
With golden beam)
That photons
Light particles
Are produced
By the fusing
The coming together
Of hydrogen atoms
And the new creation
The newly formed
Photons
Have to journey
Through the dense plasma layer
From the core.
They bounce and ricochet
They detour and backtrack
Making their way
To the surface of the sun—
A journey that takes
100,000 years.

We long for new growth
for new creation
for new songs
after burial in the soil
we long
for the best
of our ancestors
to take root in us

the love of God
the grace of light
we long for peace
we sing songs of peace
we await the peace of the world
but we bounce and ricochet
we detour and backtrack
we sing ancient songs
of war
of fear
that we should have left behind
and the journey seems
never to end.

But God bids us peace
peace at the fiery core of each heart
peace journeying
to burst out
into the world
in songs of
Light.

TIME, GOD'S HOLY CREATURE

"Time is a holy creature with which the liturgy puts one in meaningful touch... Time's sacredness is not imposed by liturgical worship. Liturgical worship discovers that sacredness and summons the assembly to take part in it."

Aidan Kavanaugh, *The Elements of Rite*

I. Word

In the beginning
before there was a world
before there was time
God spoke:
Hebrew *davar*
"word" "speech" "message"
"promise" "decision"
"story" "utterance" "acts"
"way" "manner" "cause"
Davar
God spoke
God's creating Word.
Like a river it flows
through all times,
from age to age
shaping, changing,
eroding,
building the human
landscape.
creating.
The Babylonian Talmud
says that every word
of Torah
splits into 70 languages
as many interpretations
as there are languages.

In interpreting Jeremiah 28,
Rabbi Levi said
God's word
is like a hammer
when it strikes
the rock—
sparks fly out
in every direction
as many sparks
as there are humans
each spark finding
a unique place.
God's Word—
endlessly creating
endlessly changing
From age to age.

II. Story

When we look up at the stars
in the night sky,
we are gazing not only across space,
but also across time.
We are looking at the story,
at the history,
of those stars.
We learn their names.
Though they are in the past,
they are present.
When we stand on the earth,
we are standing
not only in one specific place
but beneath our feet
are æons of time,
the story of the ancient seas
and the upheavals of the rock
of the creatures and of the people
who lived there before,
their story captured
and preserved
in the rocks
beneath our feet.
We learn their names.
Though in the past,
they are present.

In the liturgy,
through story, symbol, and image
the past is made present
the cross tells a story,
the creed,
the movement of the liturgy itself,
the prayer offices,
the liturgical year
All tell the story of God
creating, loving—
of Christ,
willing to wear the robe
of human frame—
of the Spirit,
waking dry bones from the grave.
And the story of our own being,
our own becoming,
And the becoming of the stars,
the earth, the entire cosmos,
seen and unseen.
By the loving Word of God.

III. Halakhah

Now.
is the only moment we have for living.
Shaped by the story of Christ
and the stories
of our ancestors in covenant
with God,
we live into the story of God's love.
And the prophets guide us in that
life of the present moment.
The Hebrew word for prophet
navi
comes from a root meaning
to make a sound like a bark.
The prophets bark at us
when we step off the path,
they bark
when we live counter to God's
living, creating Word.
The prophets bark
when we create or ignore
systems of greed and injustice.
The prophets bark
so that we,
and all creation,
may have abundant life
in this, the only moment we have—now.

Here, another gift from the Talmud:

Do not be daunted
by the enormity of the world's grief.
Do justly, now.
Love mercy, now.
Walk humbly, now.
You are not obligated
to complete the work,
but neither are you free to abandon it.

IV. Wisdom

Theologian Karl Rahner wrote
that the Holy Spirit
is always pressuring us from within
to evolve.
The acts that we undertake now
shape the future.
The words we speak now
continue to move out
through the universe.
For the Dakota people,
the people whose ancestors rest under our feet in Minnesota—
for the Dakota,
the word Wisdom means
"that the people may live"
and not just the people alive now
but the next seven generations, and the next seven generations, from age to age.
"That the people may live."
The Holy Spirit
is always pressuring us from within
to evolve—
to evolve into the wise, loving, creative
images of God
that God created us to be.
Our current culture
tells us that what we need
is to become capable competitors
in the world market.

But what creation
needs us to become
is loving, creative,
wise.
The team of physicists
that confirmed the existence
of the Higgs boson,
the creative field of matter,
included a classical pianist,
a philosopher,
a rock musician,
a sculptor.
The Holy Spirit is always
pressuring us from within—
to become
loving
creative
wise.
That the people may live.

V. Sabbath

At the creation
the first thing
that God named as holy
was not a mountain,
was not a spring of flowing water,
was not an animal, or the human.
The first thing that God declared to be holy
was the seventh day—
the Sabbath.
"Remember it,"
God commanded in Exodus.
"keep it,"
God commanded in Deuteronomy.
Remember it, keep it by doing
Thought and action
Mind and body
Space and time.
The Sabbath is to be a day of
joy
holiness
rest.
The Sabbath is a protest
a counter-cultural stance to the busy-ness of the world.

It is a holy time
It is, by normal standards,
a use-less day
a day on which to sanctify time,
to sanctify relationship,
with God,
with other people,
with creation—
Not one without the other.
As Christians
we have transferred the Sabbath
to the eighth day,
the Lord's day,
the day of resurrection
to be for us
a day of holy relationship
holy stories
holy song
holy time
holy place.

VI. Eucharist

Carl Gustav Jung
wrote that
at the Eucharist in the Christian liturgy
a window opens
to eternity—
Past, present, future
flow together
in one holy river of time.
In the early twentieth century,
Albert Einstein
engaged in a thought experiment:
If I sat astride a beam of light,
he pondered,
travelling at the speed of light,
how would reality appear to me?
His conclusion was
that one would exist
in an ever widening present moment
an ever-widening
Now.

In the Eucharist
past present and future
open up into an eternal moment
an eternal moment
where the stories and hopes
of our ancestors
and the dreams of creation
are fulfilled
an eternal moment
an eternal Now
The Alpha and Omega
Christ Who Is, Who Was, Who Is To Be
present among us
of whom we partake
How could we not be changed?

VII. Procession of Saints

A story from artist Gertrud Mueller Nelson:

I had my little grandson Alexander with me in late November.
The sunset was out of this world.
He came running into the house calling,
"Oma! I can see heaven! Come and see heaven!"
So we went out and watched the clouds
and he began to sing "Gloria, glooria, glooriaaa!"
And I told him that the angels were baking for Saint Nicholas Day.

When his mama came to pick him up,
the "gloria" was over, but he rushed her out
to look, and she said:
"Well, I guess the angels finished baking for today and put out the ovens."

There is a lovely mystery, says Gertrud, when I think:
MY mama told me with those November sunsets
that the "angels were baking"
And I told my Annika and my other children.
And she knows what it is all about
when Alexander tells her
"I can see heaven and the angels are baking."

There is a great procession around us
Through space
and through time
The stories of those who have lived before
the stories of all those generations not yet born
moving and singing in procession

singing the story of a loving God's creating Word
singing the story of Christ, love enrobed in human frame,
singing the story of the hallowing of human acts by the Spirit of God.
Sharing the wisdom we need
that the people may live
Barking at us to return to the path
Loving us into Abundant life

Past, present, and future
all come together
in one procession,
one story

THE YEAR IN FAITH:
A CHILDREN'S CHOIR FESTIVAL

I. Let the Whole Creation Cry

Let the whole creation cry   Glory.
Sun and Moon lift up their voice to praise God.
Night and stars lift up their voice to praise God.
Day and night praise God.
Month and year praise God.
The earth turns in its circle making day and night and praises God.
The moon turns in its circle around the earth making the lunar month and praises God.
The earth travels in its circle around the sun making the year and the seasons and praises God.
The human travels in its circle of the seasons of life from birth back to death and praises God.
The Church remembers the life of Jesus Christ in the circle of the church year and praises God.

Celebrating the church year
is like reading a storybook
that has two parts.
From Advent to Pentecost,
for six months,
we read and retell the story of Jesus:
from his mother's pregnancy to his birth,
to his teaching and healing in Galilee,
to his arrest, trial, death and resurrection in Jerusalem.
Then we hear about how Jesus came to the disciples
after he rose from the dead,
how he ascended into the heavens,
and promised to send the Holy Spirit.

On the day of Pentecost,
when the wind
and the small flames of fire
and the Holy Spirit arrive
and fill the disciples,
we come to the end of Part One.
It is important to remember
that we are telling the story
so that we can hear it again each year.
The story of Jesus' life took place over thirty-three years,
but we want to tell that story
once each year,
so we squeeze that story into six months.
We must use our imaginations
to see the story of Jesus in this way.
The Church remembers
the life of Jesus Christ
in the circle of the church year
and praises God.

II. Advent

The church year starts with Advent,
usually on the first Sunday of December
or the last Sunday in November.
It is the dark time of year.
Days are short.
Nights are long.
The sun is low and distant in the sky.
It is too cold, too dark,
for most plants to grow.
Many days are gray, like twilight.
It is a good time to pray
for light to come into the world.

Jesus said,
"I am the light of the world.
Whoever follows me
will never walk in darkness,
but will have the light of life."

And so we pray "Come."
(Advent, after all, is from a Latin word that means "coming")
And so we pray "Come."
And so we sing "O Come, O Come, Emmanuel."
And so we hang our sanctuaries with the color blue.
Blue for hope.
Blue for Mary, who was open to the will of God.
And so we light candles
to recall and to call to the light of the world.
And so we pray "Come."

We know that Jesus was born two thousand years ago.
We know that Jesus came to Bethlehem to Mary and Joseph.
This is not the coming we pray for in Advent.

We pray "Come, Lord."
We pray *Maranatha*.
We pray for Christ to come now to us.
We pray for Christ to be born in us
        in our hearts
        in our lives
so that we may be light to the world
in these dark times.

And so we pray "Come!"

III. Christmas

Now in the depth of winter
When the days are short,
and the nights so long,
In the depth of winter,
when the northern hemisphere
is so yearning for the light to return,
The midnight is torn apart
by the brightness of angels
and the shepherds hear the song of the stars
falling around them like snow.
White and gold.
White and gold.
From the deep blue of night.
Christ-mas.
The Mass of Christ.
God's promise that the night
shall not be forever,
that light will come into the world.

The very first Christmas trees
were brought into the churches
in the Middle Ages
as a part of church dramas
about the Christian life.
The trees were hung
with apples
to remind the people of the garden of Eden
and the separation from God
that had brought humans
into such a long night.

The trees were hung with apples
and hung also with
communion wafers
to remind the people of Jesus
who came into the world to bridge
that ancient separation,
Jesus, who had brought light back to the world.
Now the apples on the evergreen trees
at Christmas
have become red blown-glass balls
and the communion wafers
have been replaced by Chrismons
and straw stars.
And always they point us to the light
          that came into the world,
the light that comes into the world.
Alleluia.

IV. Lent

After the twelve days of Christmas,
After the day of Epiphany
when the great wise men of the East came to Jesus,
after we learn
through the winter days
of the various ways Jesus
    called people
    taught people
    healed people
    loved people
As the days begin to lengthen,
As we begin to feel a need to be done with winter
we enter into a time called Lent.

Beginning on Ash Wednesday
(Why ashes?
Ashes for repentance, like Job
Ashes for cleansing—ashes are an ingredient in soap, after all—)
Beginning with Ash Wednesday
for forty weekdays
we journey
forty days
a reminder
of Jesus' forty days
in the wilderness
to prepare for his mission on earth

for forty days
we journey
we repent
we pray for a clean heart
we prepare for our mission on earth
we prepare for the coming spring
we prepare for the coming Easter
for the coming newness
and Jesus journeys with us
all the way.

V. Holy Week

Toward the end of the forty day journey
of Lent
comes a most holy time:
we lift up palms and olive branches
and enter with Jesus into Jerusalem.
It is a most holy time.
Holy Week, it is called.
Last year our family had no television during this week.
This year, no meat.

The different scenes of this holy week:
    Jesus riding on a donkey entering Jerusalem
    Jesus overturning the moneylenders' tables in the temple
    Jesus eating the Passover meal with his disciples
    Jesus praying and arrested in the garden
    Jesus nailed to the cross and dying
the different pictures in our hearts and minds this holy week
are not the pictures we would imagine
of a king
no crown but thorns
no throne but the cross.

So as the week some call holy week begins with palms
and shouts of hosanna,
we,
knowing full well
how this week will end
on Good Friday,
on God's Friday,
we, knowing full well,
we pick up our palms
and shout hosanna
to the king who had no kingdom on earth
to the king who rode not a chariot, but a donkey.

"My kingdom is not of this world," said Jesus.
And we answer
Hosanna.

VI. Easter

From the way things appear on earth
when a person dies
it seems the end.
But Christ has shown us otherwise.
Spring follows winter.
Trees which dropped their leaves
and slept through the dark time
now bud and leaf again.
Crocus blossoms burst from snow.
Christ bursts from the grave.

Spring follows winter.
The sun follows the night.
Easter follows Good Friday.
Do not be afraid, said the angel at the empty tomb.
Do not be afraid, he is risen from the dead.
The dark of night is past.
The sun arises for the new day.
All shall be well.
All shall be well.

VII. The Second Part of the Story

Now after Pentecost,
usually near the month of June,
we open the storybook
of the church year
to Part Two.
In this half of the year,
we celebrate
how the story of each of our lives
and the life of the whole Church
come together with God's story,
and what God's story
in Jesus
means for our lives.
Then we begin again
with Advent,
reading the book again.
A full circle.
A full circle for praising God.
And in that story,
in that circle,
we are always held in Christ
travelling with Christ,
centered in Christ.

VIII. The Circle of the Seasons

The church year is a way of remembering the seasons of Jesus Christ's life—
birth, youth, death, rising.
It is a way of remembering the seasons of human life—
birth, youth, death, rising.
The church year is a way of remembering and praising God
through every season of the year
through every season of life.
Everything has its very own season.

HEAVEN AND EARTH IN LITTLE SPACE

There is no rose of such virtue
As is the rose that bare Jesu,
Alleluia.

For in that rose contained was
Heaven and earth in little space.
Res miranda.

By that rose we may well see
That he is God in persons three.
Pari forma.

The angels sungen the shepherds to:
"Gloria in excelsis Deo"
Gaudeamus.

Leave we all this worldly mirth.
And follow we this joyful birth.
Transeamus.

Mediæval carol

I. Heaven/Earth

II. Power/Vulnerability

III. Eternity/Time

IV. Divine/Human

V. Past/Future

VI. Sovereign/Servant

VII. Alpha/Omega

I. Heaven/Earth

Throughout the Saint John's Bible
the presence of the divine
is depicted by
the application of gold leaf—
actual thin sheets of gold
applied to the vellum pages.
At the story
of the birth of Christ
as told by Luke
the illumination for the story—
in deep midnight blues
and scarlets—
is split
by a great column
of gold leaf
splitting the night
joining the top of the page
with the center
joining heaven and earth
in the manger
the glow wakes the sky
the gold leaf angels sing
a barn harbors heaven
the holy is present
in the ordinary.

But if we look closely,
we see that the faces of the holy family
also shimmer with gold
and the shepherds behind them
and the horns on the ram
and the forehead of the donkey
and the stars
and the straw
and the stones on the ground.
The glory of God
fills all ordinary things
with the radiant light
of Christ.

II. Power/Vulnerability

In 1934
German church composer
Hugo Distler
received a commission
from the Third Reich:
to write a soldier's marching song
propagandizing the
"deep kinship" between
Germany and the soon-to-be-annexed
Austria.
Eight years later
when he was drafted to serve
in that marching army
in World War II,
Distler took his own life.
Thirty years later
Jan Bender,
church composer and student
of Distler
remembered and wanted to save
Distler's bold melody
and commissioned
Lutheran theologian and poet
Martin Franzmann
to write a Christian text
for the Distler tune.

It was during the time of
the Vietnam war.
War, again.
So Franzmann wrote
a hymn of Christ
the lowly servant
bidding us
sheathe our swords.
Christ, both Lamb and Shepherd.
Christ, God-among-us.
Christ, the Crucified One.
Powerful in weakness
A stumbling block
to those who think
they are wise.

III. Eternity/Time

Some scientists believe
that our universe
may be but one
of an infinite number
of universes
parallel to each other
or scattered
or rank after rank
extending into infinity
Some posit that
we exist simultaneously
in different universes
changed by the choices
we make.
What if…

What if,
when we make a decision
toward beauty,
we would find ourselves
in a more beautiful universe?
What if the choice is toward forgiveness
and we find ourselves
in a more forgiving universe?

What if we lean toward
compassion
and wake up in a universe that is
more peaceful and just?
Christ, you, the everlasting instant,
color all our days
all our choices
with the gold leaf
of your divinity.

IV. Divine/Human

The great hymnwriter
St. Ephrem the Syrian wrote:
"Christ clothed himself in language,
so that he might clothe us
in his mode of life."

Irenaeus of Lyons wrote
in the second century:
"In His immeasurable love,
Christ became what we are
in order to make us what he is."

This is a fractal universe.
A fractal
is a repeated pattern of sameness—
such as the smallest limbs of a tree
echoing the shape of the branches
echoing the overall shape of the tree
Or such as the orbits of electrons
around the nucleus of an atom
echoing the orbits of stars
around the central black hole of a galaxy
Or the shape of a nest
and a whirlpool
and a tornado
and the Coriolis effect.
or the shape of a river system
and the shape of

our veins and capillaries
From the smallest
to the largest
patterns of sameness
shape the universe.
From the Creation
to the Incarnation at Christmas
to the meal of bread and wine
at Christ's table
to the becoming
of Christ's people
at the meal
patterns of sameness
infuse
and shape
God's universe.
Who could but gasp,
"Emmanuel."

V. Past/Future

All these seeming opposites
come together
in the Christ
come together
in the cross:
Heaven and Earth +
Death and Life +
Divine and Human +
Time and Space +
Body and Spirit +
Abundance and Sacrifice +
Suffering and Joy +
Darkness and Light +
Past and Future +

The psalmist wrote:
God spoke one,
and I heard two.

We often regret the past.
We often fear the future.

God spoke one,
and I heard two.

But the only moment we actually have
for life in this world
for life on earth
is Now

this present instant
where past and future come together
God spoke one
and I heard two
Now is the time for justice
Now is the time for peace
Now is the time for music
Now is the time for praise
Now is the time
for the radiant gold
of divine
human
life.

VI. Sovereign/Servant

The final stanza
of the mediæval text
on which this festival
is based
is:
Leave we all this worldly mirth
And follow we this joyful birth.
Transeamus.
Transeamus.
Let us cross over
Let us cross over
to wonder,
to gratitude
let us cross over to this Christ life
let us cross over
to this life of servanthood
Let us cross over to this life
of royal personhood in humble form.
let us cross over
and actually choose
this path.

In Ursula Le Guin's fantasy book
A Wizard of Earthsea,
the young mage-in-training Ged
learns about use of power:

"The Master Summoner spoke softly
and his eyes were somber as he looked at Ged.
'You thought, as a boy, that a mage is one who can do anything.
So I thought once. So did we all.
And the truth is that as a [person's] real power grows
and [their] knowledge widens, ever the way [they] can follow grows narrower;
until at last one chooses nothing, but does only and wholly
what one <u>must</u> do . . .'"

Leave we all this worldly mirth
And follow we this joyful birth.
Transeamus.

VII. Alpha/Omega

In the Sarum rite,
the rite used in England
prior to the Reformation,
the sequence hymn for Compline
on the Feast of the Holy Name of Jesus
was as follows:

Now let us rehearse our Lord's dear titles in order:
King, Messiah,
Emmanuel, Savior,
and Lord of Sabaoth:
Consubstantial, the Way and the Life,
the Hand, Only-begotten:
Wisdom and Might, Beginning,
the Firstborn of every creature:
Alpha and Omega we name Him,
at once both the Head and the Ending:
Fountain and Source of all good,
our Advocate and Mediator:
He is the Heifer, the Lamb,
Sheep, Ram,
the Worm, Serpent, and Lion:
Mouth and Word of God,
Light, Sun, Glory,
Splendour and Image:
Blossom, Bread, Vine,
Door, Rock, Mountain
and Stone of the Corner:

Angel and Spouse of His Church,
the Shepherd,
the Priest and the Prophet:
Mighty, Immortal, Supreme,
the Lord God Omnipotent, Jesus:
These be Thy titles, Jesu:
to Thee be all honour and glory.

Transeamus.

BEYOND ALL THOUGHT AND FANTASY

I. **Beyond All Thought and Fantasy**
II. **That God Should Take Our Mortal Form**
III. **For Us**
IV. **For Us Baptized**
V. **For Us He Prayed, For Us He Taught**
VI. **By Words and Signs**
VII. **Still Seeking Not Himself, but Us**

I. Beyond All Thought and Fantasy

In the Apostle Paul's letter to the
church at Ephesus, in what is now Turkey,
Paul writes,
"I pray that you may
have the power to comprehend
with all the saints,
what is the breadth
and length
and height
and depth
and to know the love of Christ
that surpasses knowledge,
so that you may be filled
with all the fullness of God."
Fourteen centuries
after Paul wrote those words,
a German monastic, Thomas à Kempis
penned a hymn
O amor quam ecstaticus
based on this very passage from Paul's letter,
putting into song the absolute certainty,
yet mystery,
of God's love shown forth in Christ,
love "how deep, how broad, how high,
beyond all thought and fantasy."
For us faith often seems to be
something we need to know, to understand, to comprehend

And yet the word "belief" is related
to the word "Beloved."
And when we say the word
Credo,
we are speaking a compound Latin word
made up of *cor,* heart
and *do,* I give.
When we say we believe in God,
we are saying that God is the Beloved.
And when we say *credo*
we are saying
I give my heart to God.

II. That God Should Take Our Mortal Form

At six o'clock in the evening,
in many small towns and cities
across the world,
at six o'clock
the church bells toll
three sets of three rings:
the *Angelus* bell,
to commemorate the Incarnation,
to call to mind
the Word made flesh
dwelling among us.
Work stops,
in field, in town, on the street,
and the devout speak three biblical responses,
followed by three prayers:
V: The angel of the Lord declared unto Mary
(hence the name *Angelus*)
R: And she conceived of the Holy Spirit.
V: Behold the handmaid of the Lord,
R: Be it done with me according to your word.
V: And the Word was made flesh
R: And dwelt among us.

The angel announced,
but it was God who came.
As Kempis wrote:
"God sent no angel to our race…
but wore the robe of human frame."
God entered creation
as a human, made of flesh and bone

Blessing human life
blessing our bodies
blessing creation
blessing relationship
blessing us.
The *Angelus* bell
calls us to stop
and remember
to call to mind
the great and blessed mystery
of Christ's incarnation.
In the words of Irenaeus of Lyons:
"In immeasurable love
Christ became what we are
to make us
what Christ is."

III. For Us

Theologian and priest Thomas Berry
wrote that
"nothing in the universe
exists without communion,"
nothing exists
without at least two things
coming together—
atoms, electrons,
dark energy,
dark matter
"Nothing in the universe
exists without communion."
For us.
"For us"
Thomas à Kempis wrote
in his hymn "O Love, How Deep"
Eleven times he wrote
"For us"
(Benjamin Webb the translator, even more . . .)
Eleven times "for us"
Nobis.
Pro nobis.
plural.
not just "for me"
For *us*.

"Nothing in the universe exists without communion."
If God is love
as the scriptures declare
If God is Trinity
as the church teaches
then the hallmark
the sign
the evidence of being in God
of living in God
of being infused with God
of giving our heart to God
is existing in loving community
in compassionate coming together
in divine communion
with all people
with all creation.
"Nothing in the universe
exists without communion."
For Us.
Plural.

IV. For Us Baptized

In the western Church
we celebrate
two major feast days after Christmas—
Epiphany and
The Baptism of Our Lord.
In the Orthodox church
this is one holy day—
the Theophany, the appearing of God,
and a part of the liturgy for this feast
is the Blessing of Water,
for Christ in entering
the rivers of the Jordan
blessed all the earth's waters
with his divine radiance.
The Orthodox Blessing of Water
on the feast of the Theophany
includes this prayer:

Today the grace of the Holy Spirit has descended
on the waters in the likeness of a dove...
Today the clouds from heaven moisten humankind
with showers of justice.
Today the waters of the Jordan are changed into healing
at the presence of the Lord.
Today the whole universe is watered
by mystical streams.
Today the sins of mortals are blotted out
by the water of the Jordan.
Today the bitter water is changed at the hand of Moses
to sweetness by the presence of the Lord.
Today has paradise been opened to us,
and the Sun of Righteousness has shone for us.

V. For Us He Prayed, For Us He Taught

Thomas à Kempis wrote a third stanza
to "O Love, How Deep"
a stanza not often included
in today's hymnals:

> "Nor willed he only to appear
> His pleasure was to tarry here;
> And God in man with us would be
> The space of thirty years and three."

Christ tarried among us for,
it is said,
thirty-three years,
a double Trinity of time,
teaching, healing,
living, weeping
eating, drinking
sighing, praying.
His life was sculpted by prayer
a constant reconnecting
to the divine source of all
a quiet reordering
a conscious diving into God-consciousness
that did not take Christ
out of the world
where he had willed to tarry
but deeper *into* the world,
its pain and problems,
its joys and singing.
Prayer does not help us escape the world
Prayer helps us live deeply in the world.

A story from the rabbinic tradition:

A rabbi, upon entering a room,
saw his son deep in prayer.
In the corner,
stood a cradle with a baby crying.
The rabbi asked his son,
"Can't you hear?
There's a baby crying in this room."
The son said,
"Father, I was lost in God."
And the rabbi said,
"One who is lost in God
can see the very fly
crawling up the wall."

VI. By Words and Signs

Sister Mary Evelyn Jegen
was a sister of Notre Dame de Namur
she taught elementary school
she taught college.
For most of her adult life
she worked with great resolve
for peace and justice
in Rome
in India
in the United States
she worked for Bread for the World
she worked for Pax Christi
and she discovered
and practiced
the art of
benevolent glancing
benevolent glancing
the art of attentiveness
the art of kind prayerfulness
the art of care for the stranger
Benevolent glances.
How much the
people in the world
need benevolent glances!
The healing power
of benevolent glances.

How the creatures
the marshes
the mountains
the rivers
need benevolent glances!
How the world needed
the benevolent glances of Christ
the benevolent words of Christ
the touch of Christ
the acts of Christ.
O love, how deep
how broad, how high...
Perhaps
perhaps
we will discover
that a part
of our vocation
as the body of Christ
is the vocation of
benevolent glances.

VII. Still Seeking Not Himself, but Us

O love, how deep
how broad
how high.
Pro nobis.
For us.
Christ came among us
changing the waters of the Jordan
into healing.
Christ came teaching
praying
sheltering healing
ministering with
benevolent acts
benevolent glances.
Not with chariot and spear
but with patience
not with power and coercion
but with a loving call
How much easier,
Dorothy Sayers wrote, "far better
To make but one resplendent miracle,
Lean through the cloud, lift the right hand of power
And with a sudden lightning smite the world perfect.
Yet this was not God's way, Who had the power,
But set it by, choosing the cross, the thorn,
The sorrowful wounds. Something there is, perhaps,
That power destroys in passing, something supreme,
To whose great value in the eyes of God
That cross, that thorn, and those five wounds bear witness."

We give our heart
we give our trust
to the God
whose way is love
compassion
benevolent glances
healing creation
healing the human heart
and drawing us all in
under tender
sheltering
wings.

JESUS CHRIST, YESTERDAY, TODAY, AND FOREVER

Christ is the image of the invisible God,
the firstborn of creation;
for in him all things
in heaven and on earth were created,
things visible and invisible,
whether thrones or dominions or rulers or powers—
all things have been created
through him and for him.
He himself is before all things
and in him all things hold together.
He is the head of the body, the Church;
he is the beginning,
the firstborn from the dead,
so that he might come to have
first place in everything.
For in him
all the fullness of God
was pleased to dwell,
and through him
God was pleased
to reconcile to himself
all things,
whether on earth or in heaven,
by making peace
through the blood
of his cross.

Colossians 1:15-20

I. Image of the Invisible God

II. Firstborn of Creation

III. In Him All Things in Heaven and on Earth Were Created

IV. In Him All Things Hold Together

V. He Is the Beginning, the Firstborn of the Dead

VI. For in Him All the Fullness of God Was Pleased to Dwell

I. Image of the Invisible God

Christ is Alpha and Omega
He is Beginning and End
He is our starting point
And our destination.
Franciscan Richard Rohr
writes:
"If God is Trinity,
and Jesus is the Face of God,
then it is a benevolent universe.
God is not someone to be afraid of,
but is the Ground of Being
and on our side."
God is a loving God
and Jesus while on earth
and the Risen Christ
and the Spirit of God
have been trying to
convince humans of this
for millennia.

From the heart of God
to the heart of Christ
to our heart.
God is love—
God is a relationship of love—
full of mercy
and compassion.
And Jesus is
the Face
of God.

II. Firstborn of Creation

The Jesuit paleontologist and theologian
Teilhard de Chardin wrote that
There is no matter
without spirit.
In quantum physics,
Bell's theorem posits
that all particles of matter are connected
at a fundamental and deep level.
Matter and spirit.
Douglas firs in the Pacific Northwest
nurture their seedlings
by sharing much-needed carbon
the giant trees could easily
consume for themselves
Spirit and matter.
White rats will work to free
a trapped and caged compatriot,
even ignoring chocolate
in an adjacent cage.
There is no matter without spirit.
Rocks vibrate
with the memory
of all of the earth's creating.
Matter and spirit.

And in Christ
God revealed
God's face—
in matter
in earth
in elements
in water and bones and flesh—
God's self-revelation
the Image of the Invisible God
in a human body
capable of growth
capable of suffering
capable of relationship
capable of compassion
Matter and spirit.
the Firstborn of creation
the Firstborn of the Dead
the Firstfruits of them that sleep
God's face.
Gloria.

III. In Him All Things in Heaven and on Earth Were Created

Anytime the Hebrew Scriptures
repeat something three times
it is wise to pay attention—
"And one seraph called to another
and said:
Holy, holy, holy...
Kadosh, kadosh, kadosh!
The whole earth is full
is full of God's glory!"

In 1573 Francisco de Holanda
depicted in an illustration
the creation of the world:
In a large red circle of fire
a white equilateral triangle
with the Greek letters Alpha and Omega
is centered
And cascading down from it
is an elongated triangle
inscribed with the gilt words
Fiat lux—
Let there Be Light,
and this triangle funnels light
into the chaotic
water- and cloud-cloaked
world.

The triangle
the Alpha and Omega
actually enters the creation
God's energy is funneled
taking form
God's Threefold Self
enters creation
the spirit hovering over the waters
As Pierre Teilhard de Chardin wrote:
"By means of all created things,
the divine assails us,
penetrates us, and molds us.
We imagine the Divine
as distant and inaccessible,
when in fact
we live steeped in its burning layers."

And it is holy.
Kadosh, kadosh, kadosh!
The whole earth
is full of God's glory!

IV. In Him All Things Hold Together

When the monks of St. John's Abbey
enter the abbey church for worship
they enter by twos.
They bow first to the altar
then they turn
and bow to each
other.
"You too are
the dwelling place of God,"
they are saying with their bodies.
God is Holy.
You are Holy.
We are Holy.
Kadosh, kadosh, kadosh.
Christ moves through all things
ta panta—
all things.
And thus we are all connected—
not just to God
not just to Christ
but to each other

Fingertips pressed against
a pane of frosted glass
appear to be
five separate oval forms
but if one looks
from a different
vantage point
one sees
that they are actually
five fingers
and those fingers connected to a hand
and that hand to an arm
and that arm to a body
and that body to a head.
In Christ all things—
ta panta—
all things hold together.
Blessed.

V. He Is the Beginning, the Firstborn of the Dead

Jesus said, “Unless a grain of wheat
falls into the ground and dies . . . ”
For something new
to come into being
something has to die
something has to change
something has to be let go
This is life in space and time.
(A computer-generated
DNA molecule
when viewed axially
looks like a crown of thorns.)
Jesus said,
“Unless a grain of wheat
falls into the ground and dies . . . ”
Jesus, Incarnate Love,
Face of God,
allowed his deep
and intimate connection
to the God of Love
to take flesh
in every aspect of his
life on earth:
relationship
connectedness
compassion—

even if it led to suffering
even if it led to death.
And where anger could have justly been
Christ's response,
Christ healed.
And where righteous indignation or hatred
could have been justified,
Christ forgave.
The Face of God.
Incarnate Love.
And love does not deplete itself.
Like the light of the Paschal candle
passed from candle to candle
at the Great Vigil of Easter,
light gradually filling
the whole temple.
Love is not diminished
when divided and borrowed.
Something new has come into being
in the darkness.
Filling the whole temple.
Love does not deplete itself.

VI. For in Him All the Fullness of God Was Pleased to Dwell

We must understand this:
If we are open to Christ
If we have made space in ourselves
for Christ
we become
capax Christi
capable of Christ
we become
capax universi
capable of the universe
"Greater things than these
you will do," said Jesus.
From the heart of God
through the heart of Christ
to our heart
a letting go
a becoming
a new thing.
We must ask this:
Of what use is it
that we say we believe
that Christ was born
lived died and rose from the dead
if we do not also let go
if we do not also
rise from our old selves
and become new
become more
become transformed
become Christ?
Life in Christ
is not a Director's Circle
with reserved parking
and special privileges
but rather

a radical willingness
to let go
to become new
to become more
to become Christ
to become Incarnate Love.
In the Hasidic Jewish tradition,
it is said,
"Every person has around them
a legion of angels
proclaiming:
'Behold the Image of God!'"

Prayer

O Incomprehensible God,
You loved us from before all worlds
and from your heart
You called all things into being.
Blessed are You for life;
blessed are You for relationship;
blessed are You for the Christ,
present with You from the beginning
and still shaping and filling this world,
urging us, beckoning us,
cajoling us to become more.
May we visibly become your image
in this world,
co-creators with You,
loving Your creation
to its completion,
through Christ and Your Spirit,
who with You are making all things new,
unto all ages of ages.
Amen

JOURNEYS

I. Journey in God

There are many journeys in life
we are on a journey of becoming
we are on a journey of faith
Each day is a journey
we awaken
we breathe
we open our eyes
we stretch
a new journey begins
How good to begin
the day's journey
with gratitude
with prayer
with an acknowledgement
that our waking
our breathing
our seeing
come from the generous abundance
of the Creating and Sustaining God
"in whom we live and move
and have our being"
Our journey is in God
whether we are aware or not
whether we believe it or not
There is no place
where God is not.

How good to walk
through the journey of the day
aware and awake
aware of God's presence
awake to the God-light in each person
that we encounter
How good to give thanks
for these,
all our companions
How good to walk through the day
seeing the sister trees
and the brother rocks
on our journey
All emerging from and sustained by
the Heart of God
How good and pleasant it is...

II. Journey with Purpose

People sense deep down
that there is more to life
than making money
and paying bills
Some reach a point
in life
when all seems
dry and barren
food loses savor
dawn loses pleasure
extreme experiences entice
But even these
do not suffice.
shopping
planning
acquiring
we discern
only temporarily satisfy
Humans of all ages
find themselves
thirsting
for the reality
underlying reality

It is a thirst
that will not be quenched.
and, often
we search for the key
in all the wrong places
while patiently
God
waits

III. Journey with Christ

In the first room
of the National Civil Rights Museum
in Memphis, Tennessee,
there is on display
an old yellowed poster:

TO BE SOLD & LET
BY PUBLIC AUCTION
on MONDAY the 18th of MAY 1829
Under the Trees

FOR SALE
The Three Following Slaves:
HANNIBAL
WILLIAM
NANCY

Also For Sale:
FINE RICE, GRAM, PADDY, BOOKS, MUSLINS . . .
And the fine well-known horse
BLUCHER

How important for
Hannibal
and William
and Nancy
to know that they had a companion
on their journey
on their journey of separation
Christ had walked before
on their journey of uncertainty
Christ had walked before
on their journey of sadness and sorrow and danger
Christ had walked before

How important for all people
to know
we have a companion
who has walked this way before
we are never on this pilgrimage
alone
And despair need have no
power over us
For we are accompanied
in all walks of life
by the steadfast love
of the Living
Christ.

IV. Journey through Wilderness

A poem by Robert Frost, “In Hardwood Groves”:

The same leaves over and over again!
They fall from giving shade above
To make one texture of faded brown
And fit the earth like a leather glove.

Before the leaves can mount again
To fill the tree with another shade,
They must go down past things coming up.
They must go down into the dark decayed.

They must be pierced by flowers and put
Beneath the feet of dancing flowers.
However it is in some other world
I know that this is the way in ours.

“They must go down into the dark decayed...”
Pablo Picasso said:
“Every act of creation is
first of all an act of destruction.”
The life journey
takes us into the wilderness,
into “the dark decayed,”
where we can set aside
those things that enchain us,
encumber and restrain us.
Down into the dark decayed,
where the small hard, dried seed
can begin its transformation,
where we can be pressured to Become.

A story from the Hasidic tradition:
A disciple asks the rebbe,
Why does the Torah tell us
to place these words upon your hearts?
Why does it not tell us
to place the holy words in our hearts?
The rebbe answers:
It is because as we are,
our hearts are closed and hard,
and we cannot place
the holy words in our hearts.
So we place them on top of our hearts
And there they stay until
one day our heart breaks,
and the holy words fall in.

V. Journey in Community

In the years
1898 and 1899,
composer Edward Elgar
composed an orchestral work—
the *Enigma Variations,*
which he wrote to honor
his closest friends and beloved family,
creating for each person
a musical movement that was a variation
on a theme.
These were the people
who had prepared the soil
for Elgar,
who had helped create
the conditions in which
the seed of creativity in him could flourish.
We are all connected here—
quantum physics and biology
show us this simple fact
We are all connected.
This we live out
each time we gather at communion together
for Christ's one bread,
for Christ's one cup
This we live out
in singing God's story together,
breathing together,
vibrating together,
becoming one.

We are all together here
preparing the soil for each other
preparing for the great transformation.
Perhaps in gratitude
and in wonder
we should
write our own *Enigma Variations*
a poem for each person
or a sketch
or a quilt square
a garden plot
for each person
who has come into our lives
and helped
prepare the soil
for our planting.
For we are all connected here.

VI. Journey to Christ-likeness

We are on the path
through the wilderness
travelling in God,
accompanied by Christ,
driven by the Spirit,
those before us
and around us
have prepared the soil
God has brought water
to the wilderness
and we will emerge transformed
to live in the world
as Christ,
radiant with love,
mercy,
compassion.

Fourteenth century mystic Meister Eckhart wrote:
"The seed of God is in us:
Pear seeds grow into pear trees.
Hazel seeds grow into hazel trees.
And God seeds,
into God."

VII. Journey in the Spirit

Each person
is a unique, never-to-be-repeated
gift to the universe.
And the seeds of God are in us.
Who has God brought
each one of us here to be?
What gifts do each one of us
uniquely have
that the universe needs?
Christ said,
"I am the Vine;
you are the Branches."
Now, there are two layers
in the bark
of a tree or a vine:
The *xylem* which transports
water and nutrients
upward
from the root to the branches
and leaves;
And the *phloem,*
which transports
sugars and other nutrients
from photosynthesis
downward
from the leaves to the root.
The leaves need the root;
the root benefits from the leaves.

What are we becoming
on this journey of life,
this journey in the Heart of God,
this journey of time,
this journey with and into Christ?
What are we sending
back to God
from our leaves?
What are our gifts,
our talents,
our fruits?
Karl Rahner wrote that
the Holy Spirit
is always pressuring us
from within
to evolve.
"Very truly, I tell you,
unless a grain of wheat
falls into the ground and dies,
it remains just a single grain
But if it dies,
it bears much fruit."

RISE, HEART

Rise heart; thy Lord is risen. Sing his praise
Without delayes,
Who takes thee by the hand, that thou likewise
With him mayst rise:
That, as his death calcined thee to dust,
His life may make thee gold, and much more, just.

Awake, my lute, and struggle for thy part
With all thy art.
The crosse taught all wood to resound his name,
Who bore the same.
His stretched sinews taught all strings, what key
Is best to celebrate this most high day.

Consort both heart and lute, and twist a song
Pleasant and long:
Or, since all musick is but three parts vied
And multiplied,
O let they blessed Spirit bear a part,
And make up our defects with his sweet art.

George Herbert, "Easter"

I. Rise heart; thy Lord is risen

II. Who takes thee by the hand

III. That thou likewise with him mayst rise

IV. That, as his death calcined thee to dust

V. His life may make thee gold

VI. And much more, just.

I. Rise heart; thy Lord is risen

We see the graveclothes lying there
We see the stone rolled away
We see the brightness of the angel.
"Rise heart; thy Lord is risen."
Ah, sheer delight.
We see that we have become
new people
transformed people
resurrection people
For Christ is risen
And we, too, shall rise.

When artist Henri Matisse
was painting out-of-doors
he would draw a line
on the ground
around his feet
so that he could again find
the perspective
from which he had been painting
to remind himself where he stood.

Perhaps we should draw a line around our feet here
here where we see the graveclothes
here where we see the stone rolled away
here where we see the angel
draw a line around our feet
to remind ourselves where we stand
to find again our perspective
our perspective as
people of resurrection
to see as
people of resurrection
to live as people of resurrection
draw a line around our feet
to remind ourselves
that we are already standing
have always been standing
in God's garden.

II. Who takes thee by the hand

At the same time
that we are celebrating
Easter
our Jewish sisters and brothers
are celebrating
Passover—
God taking Israel
by the hand
and leading them
out of Egypt—
Egypt—
Mitzrayim in the Hebrew scriptures.
But *mitzrayim* means not only Egypt
mitzrayim also means
"narrow places"
God leading Israel
out of "narrow places"
and at Passover seders
around the world
Jews reflect
on their "narrow places"
of the past year—

things that are confining them
limiting them
enslaving them
keeping them from fullness.
The risen Christ
reaches out to us
in our *mitzrayim*
our narrow places
and offers to accompany us
on the journey
to lead us out
of our narrow places
toward the east
toward the new day
toward the dawn.

III. That thou likewise with him mayst rise

French poet Charles Péguy
wrote,
"We must always tell what we see.
Above all, and this is more difficult,
we must always see what we see."
Luke the gospelteller
tells of an encounter
on the road to Emmaus
an encounter
with the risen Christ Jesus.
Two of Jesus' disciples
walk on the road
later on that first Easter day
burdened and blinded
by their frail human hopes
saddened and disappointed
by Jesus' death and leavetaking.
Jesus joins them,
walks with them,
speaks with them.
They do not recognize him.
"Above all, and this is more difficult,
we must always see what we see."

But we know the story—
we know that Jesus made himself known
in the breaking of the bread
we know the story
we know that we are
people of the resurrection
we have marked
where we are standing in God's garden
we can see with Easter eyes
we can see what see:
Christ walking with us
out of narrow places
present in the Word
present in the gathering
present in the stranger
present in the world
we can see Christ
who takes us by the hand
that we likewise
with him
may rise.

IV. That, as his death calcined thee to dust

In the ancient process
of alchemy,
the goal was to
transform base matter
into gold,
a metaphor
for the becoming
of the human soul.
One stage in the process
was called
calcination.
As poet-priest George Herbert penned,
"That as his death calcined thee to dust,
His life may make thee gold…"
Calcination is when things fall apart,
a necessary stage in becoming.
Calcination is the dark night of the soul
separation
anxiety fear
everything stripped of external distractions
down to the essence.

In the dark night,
wrote John of the Cross,
in the dark night,
ah—sheer delight
Christ came to him
In the dark of the tomb
newness is knit together.
In the dark of the midnight
God comes to birth.
In the dark of the soil
seed bursts into life.
God and possibility are there
in the dark times.
Ah, sheer delight.

V. His life may make thee gold

Out of darkness—
new life
new day
new people.
Christ reaches out
with his wounded hands
and bids us rise
to newness
to step out
over the gates of death
and become what he is—
resurrected
new
gold.
In the illuminations of Hildegard von Bingen
the Divine is depicted
by gold.
In the handwritten pages of the
St. John's Bible,
God is present throughout
as gold.
In Orthodox Christian icons
the background field
is gold,
God's presence
God's reality

God's time.
As God's resurrection people
we become infused with gold
infused with the holy
infused with the divine.
Each one of us unique
each one needed by the universe
each one precious in God's sight.
God and the universe
conspire together
to give each of us the chance
to become gold
to become the ultimate person
God created each one to be.
Rabbi Zusya said:
"In the world to come,
I shall not be asked,
'Why were you not Moses?'
I shall be asked,
'Why were you not Zusya?'"

VI. And much more, just.

In the fourth century
Helena, the mother of Emperor Constantine,
traveled to Jerusalem
and found
what she believed to be
the True Cross,
the cross on which Jesus
was crucified.
She sent the nails from the cross
by ship to her son Constantine—
who melted them down
to make a bit
for the bridle
of his war-horse.

Who are we becoming
as resurrection people?
What do we do with the gifts of the Risen Christ?
What do we do with the sheer delight
of being freed
from the dark times
the narrow places
from fear and death?
How do we see differently?
Who are we becoming?
St. Augustine wrote:
"Become yourself
the glory that you sing of."
The Orthodox icon
of the resurrection
shows the Risen Christ
reaching out to raise
Adam and Eve,

helping them cross the abyss,
reaching out to raise
all of humanity.
How do we live as people of the resurrection?
Ah, sheer delight—
Becoming ourselves
the glory
that we sing of.

Closing Prayer

Let us pray.

O loving God, O risen Christ, O comforting Spirit,
whose love no word can express
whose care no mind can grasp:
as daylight fades around us
and your blessed dark surrounds us,
take us by the hand—
your beloved people—
and hold us in your warm embrace
through this night of rest
and into the waking day,
that we may live and breathe and move in you
giving glory to you
as your resurrected people
always held in your loving embrace.
Amen

PRAISE AND THANKSGIVING

I. A Galaxy Is an Activity

A galaxy is not a thing
A galaxy is an activity
What seem to be "arms"
of the galaxy
are density waves
areas of compression
where new stars are being
created
A galaxy is an activity,
a relationship,
a communion,
a giving and receiving
a birthing-forth
Just as the Trinity
is not a thing
but rather an activity
and activity of communion,
of divinity,
of relationship,
of conversation
of giving and receiving
of birthing-forth.

The famous icon
of the Trinity
by Rublev
is also called by another name:
the Sacred Conversation
a loving exchange
between three aspects
of God—
for communion
is the essence of Being
loving is what
holds the universe
together
loving communion
births forth stars
and new worlds
and new being.

II. Know Before Whom You Stand

Above the ark
which houses the Torah scrolls
in Jewish synagogues
are the words
"Know before whom you stand."
Know before whom
you stand.
And the One before whom
we stand
is the Creator of being itself.
We stand in worship
before the Source of All Being.
I Am.
The letters that make up
the Holy Name of God—
"ehyeh-asher-ehyeh"
are the very sound of heartbeat
"ehyeh-asher-ehyeh"
they are like breathing in and out
"ehyeh-asher-ehyeh"
the very sound of breath
God's name is Life
God's Name is what is making our heart beat
God's Name
"ehyeh-asher-ehyeh"

God's Name
is what is moving us
to breathe
You Are. You Are. You Are.
I Am. I Am. I Am.
Abraham Heschel wrote:
"Just to be is a blessing."
Just to live is holy."
Let us give God
praise
with our very heartbeat
with our very breath
to
I Am.

III. The Vine and the Branches

I Am. You Are. I Am. You Are.
"I am the vine;
You are the branches,"
spoke Christ.
Our very Being
our energy,
our inspiration
comes from God in Christ.
And with these words
we are all reminded
very clearly reminded
by the Anointed One
that we are also thus
all connected one to another
This branch doesn't have this special place,
This branch doesn't receive different sustenance
than the rest
All are connected
to each other
by Christ the Vine.

In what was Buchenwald concentration camp
there is now a memorial marker
in the ground—
to remember.
Snow never rests atop this marker
for it is kept at all times
at 98.6° Fahrenheit
the temperature of all humans
the temperature of all those
we might be tempted to regard
as being different from us
it is the temperature of all those
whose hearts beat
"ehyeh-asher-ehyeh"
with the Name of God.
The love of God lives in community
in the life of the tree
all loved
all sustained
all tended, all nourished
through all seasons of life.

IV. Singing Truth

What we sing together
shapes us
the words, carried by melody,
go deep into ourselves
and form us,
form our ideas
form our faith
both as individuals
and as the Body of Christ.
The words we sing together
matter.
And so hymnwriters
work very hard
to make sure
the words we sing together
are true.
So that we are not singing untruths into ourselves
into each other
into the universe.
Great hymns
sung over and over again
over a lifetime
go deep into memory
to sustain us
to lift us
to enhearten us
when we cannot
find the words ourselves.

Two years after having been robbed
of all his possessions
while a student
during the Thirty Years War,
Georg Neumark
was finally offered a permanent position
after living in hunger and need
for two years,
and in response
he wrote these confident words
"If you but trust in God to guide you"
for us to sing
400 years later
to sing
in faith and trust
of the never-failing
presence of
God.

V. Who Was This Jesus?

Who was this Jesus
we call Christ,
the Anointed One?
Who is this who said *I Am*?
        I am the Vine
        I am the Gate
        I am the Bread of Life
        I am the Light of the World
Who is this
at whose Name
every knee should bend?
We know Christ Jesus
was steeped in divinity
one with God
the Breath,
the Heartbeat,
of creation.
We know Jesus
was compassion,
excluding no one,
having mercy on all.
We know
he set aside time
to be alone in prayer.

He sat at table
with the whole spectrum
of people he met.
He healed people who were outside
the circle of acceptability.
He taught in stories.
He wept at his friend's death.
He suffered with those
who were suffering.
He asked hard questions.
He challenged the values
of his society.
He loved without promise of return.
And so when we pray,
"Come, Lord"
when we sing
"Give me Jesus"
we are praying into our lives
all that Jesus Christ is:
compassion, discernment,
mercy, joy at friendship,
suffering with the suffering.
We are praying into our lives
the ability to love
without promise of return.

VI. There Is a Rhythm to Life

There is a rhythm to life.
Evening is followed by night
is followed by day
is followed by evening
is followed by night.
Autumn is followed by
Winter is followed by
Spring.
Lives grow, flourish,
Ebb, wane.
Generations appear,
Generations pass away.
Galaxies take shape
Galaxies collide.
Stars burst into light
Stars collapse
New stars are birthed forth.
And shining on us still
the light from the now gone stars
And echoing in us still
the songs and wisdom
of generations now past.

And underlying all
the rhythm of God's Holy Name
"ehyeh-asher-ehyeh"
Underlying all—
the rhythm of the heartbeat of God
that brings all things to light
cradles them gently back to sleep
whispers them back to daylight.
There is a rhythm to life,
the seasons teach us
generations teach us
day and night teach us.
And underneath it all—
the loving heart of God.

WHERE CHARITY AND LOVE PREVAIL

I. **Where**
II. **Charity**
III. **And**
IV. **Love**
V. **Are**
VI. **There**
VII. **God**
VIII. **Is**

I. Where

We are earth *adamah*
we are breath *ruach* spirit
we are earth
with breath
Adam:
dalet-mem
the Hebrew letters
blood:
dalet-mem
the Hebrew letters
earth and blood
with breath.
All that we know
of the world
is mediated by
our bodies.
Our brains
and our skin
develop from the same
embryonic tissue—
the primary ectoderm.

All that we know
is mediated
by our bodies—
these good
and miraculous
and beautiful
temples of God.
All that we know
of the world
we know
by hearing
by tasting
by smelling
by seeing
by touching.
We are earth.
We are breath.

II. Charity

Compassion
Is not
the same
As Pity.
Pity is related
to the word
piety
which means
duty.
Compassion
cum patior
means
to suffer with.
In Hebrew
it is *rachamim*
literally,
to feel in one's womb.
In Greek,
splagchnizomai
to feel
in one's bowels.
To literally feel
the pain of others
in one's body

to suffer *with*
in these bodies
of earth
and breath.
It is to thirst
when others thirst
to mourn
when others mourn
to cry out
when others cry out
to feel the rocks
and thorns
on shoeless feet…

III. And

Jewish philosopher
Martin Buber
defined
two different ways
of seeing ourselves
in the world:
Ich/Du— I and Thou—
and *Ich/Es*—I and It—
I and It
sees the world outside of self
as "It"
as objects
as separate.
I and Thou
sees the world
its rocks, its trees, its creatures
other people
and God
as Thou
as connected
as beings with whom,
not with which,
with whom
we can have relationship

related
with whom
we can suffer
with whom
we can work
with whom
we can remember
with whom
we can hope
with whom
we can celebrate
with whom
we can sing
and dance.

IV. Love

A tale from Attar of Nishapur:

> The lover knocked at the door of his beloved.
> "Who knocks?" said the beloved, from within.
> "It is I," said the lover.
> "Go away. This house will not hold you and me."
>
> The rejected lover went away into the desert.
> There he meditated for months on end, pondering
> the words of the beloved.

Finally he returned and knocked at the door again.
"Who knocks?"
"It is you."

The door was immediately opened.

V. Are

Back in the nineteenth century
Justus von Liebig
identified the three primary
macronutrients
in soil—
nitrogen, phosphorus, and potassium
and claimed
these three elements
were all a plant needs
to grow and thrive.
But we since
have learned
that there is
a whole ecosystem
in the soil
rhizobacteria
fungi
springtails
tardigrades
calcium boron
earthworms,
voles and moles
that are necessary
to the life of the plants

And the carbon dioxide
that we exhale—
needed for photosynthesis
when the plants breathes out water
and oxygen
oxygen which fires our brains
our thoughts
And the bogs breathe in
and filter water
and the rivers breathe
the water into motion
and air breathes in the water
to rain
and the leaves breathe in the water
to make food
from sunlight.
Mitakuye oyasin
say the Lakota:
"all my relations."
"I am the vine,
you are the branches,"
said Christ.

VI. There

Teilhard de Chardin
wrote that
If God is love,
then each act of love
increases God's sway
on the universe.
Into this
world
came Jesus,
earth and breath
blood and bone
filled with holiness
filled with the glory of God
living out
the
I—Thou
with God
with the shoeless
with those
with the hand on the plow
with the suffering

with the song-filled
with the outcast
with friends
with pagans
with all
with us.

VII. God

There is an ancient description
of God:
God is
an intelligible circle
whose center
is everywhere
and circumference,
nowhere.
Every time
we try to limit
God,
we find ourselves
grasping at a horizon
we can never
reach.
The accepted Gospels
report that
Jesus called God
Abba, Father
Julian of Norwich called God
Mother
John of the Cross,
Beloved
Saint John,
Love.

Every time
we try to limit
God's love,
we find ourselves
gathered at a feast
with all the people
we have chosen not to love,
and the
host at the table
embraces us all
with wounded hands.

VIII. Is

Earth
Breath
Heart
Hearth
Here in these
bodies
of earth and blood
bone and breath
we live
held in
the loving center
who is everywhere,
whose circumference
is nowhere.
we live
seeing Christ
in the eyes
of our companions on earth,
feeling in our bones
the suffering of the world,
tasting in our tears
our common source
hearing in our songs
the mystery that reason cannot grasp,
the mystery the universe groans
in awaiting:
where charity
and love
are
there God is.

Prayer

O God, Life of all life,
Breath of all that breathes,
You have made us humans from humus;
You have woven all of us together
in a living vine of life.
Open our ears to hear Your song;
open our eyes to see your Christ in those around us;
open our hearts to love without fear;
open our hands to reach out in healing;
open our lips to sing out beauty,
For You desire the coming to fulfillment
of all things in Christ Jesus
through
the Holy Spirit,
to whom with You
be glory and honor
now and to all ages of ages.
Amen

WE BELIEVE IN THE HOLY SPIRIT

I. We believe in the Holy Spirit . . . the giver of life . . .

When we come to the Third Article
of the two primary creeds that we confess,
whether the Apostles' Creed
or the Nicene Creed,
when we come to the Third Article,
we essentially encounter the question
"Why do the first two articles of the Creed matter?
What do they have to do with life?
What life do we live in response
to God as the Creator
and to God as the Christ?"
The life *of* and *in*
and *by* the Holy Spirit.
"We believe in the Holy Spirit, the giver of life . . .
and the life of the world to come."
This third section begins and ends with
life.
The life of the Spirit.
And the life of the Spirit transforms us
causes us to evolve, to change,
to become *more.*
Theologian Karl Rahner wrote that
We are pressured from within by the Holy Spirit
to evolve.
If we picture God the Creator as an ineffable Ocean,
and Christ as a River passing through and bounded by earth,
then the Spirit is the Rain that brings
that life-giving water
to the parched
and distant places

transforming the land
growing green
producing luscious fruit.
Or, if God is pictured as Fire,
and Christ is the Light from that Fire,
then the Spirit is the Heat
that warms
and transforms
and bakes
and melts away dross, creating something new.
Have you noticed?
Our hymns and prayers to the Spirit
do not ask for something
to be done
in our place
in our stead:
our prayers to the Spirit
ask that we continue to be
pressured from within
to evolve,
to change
to become the
vessel of God
that the
universe
needs us
to be.

II. ...who has spoken through the prophets

In our own lives
there is a trinity
of relationship
always in movement:
our relationship
to ourself.
our relationship
to God.
our relationship to the world:
to other people,
to all of creation, all our brothers and sisters.
As a child we turn in a circle
and we see that we are
always the center,
everything turns around us.
Me.
If we are fortunate enough
to be immersed in a bigger story,
often through a faith tradition,
we add a relationship:
to the Source of All Things, to God.
Me. And God.
But it cannot stop there:
God's Word comes to us
through the prophets,
those who hear the "silent sigh."

The prophets, who,
as Abraham Heschel said,
"while the world is at ease and asleep...
feel the blast from heaven."
The prophets, stirred by the Word of God,
pressured from within
by the Spirit of God
call us to awaken
and to become aware
of the third relationship
in our trinity:
our relationship to the creation
and all its creatures
our sisters and brothers of every species and kind.
The Word of God
spoken by the prophets
is the power of the Spirit
pressuring us from within,
to become more,
to live out the Trinity
in great love for self,
great love for God, and
great love for Other.

III. We believe in one holy catholic and apostolic church

In the monastery that
Saint Benedict founded
in the hills at Subiaco, Italy,
there is a fourteenth century fresco
depicting Mary, the Mother of the Church,
sheltering all the people
gathered and
protected under the folds of her
beautiful brocade cloak.

In one of Hildegard von Bingen's
visions
she described
a woman, the Great Mother,
an imposing figure
in gold and blue
who holds the people
of the Church
to her bosom,
at the level of her heart,
Mother Church,
sheltering the people
with her wings.
When we proclaim
in the creed
that we believe in one holy catholic and apostolic Church,
we are stating
that we do not live
as the solitary child at the center of her world,
nor as "I have a relationship with God,
the rest of you go away please,"

but as a person
immersed in a bigger story
connected by that story
to all people,
to all creatures,
all things.
The Holy Spirit is pressuring us
from within
to become more,
to become willing participants
in a bigger story
shot through with the blue of compassion
shot through with the gold of divinity
sheltered as community
under the golden wings of God.

IV. We acknowledge one baptism for the forgivness of sins

Nigerian writer
Chinua Achebe,
wrote,
"Only the story
can continue beyond the war
and the warrior...
It is the story that saves
our progeny
from blundering like blind beggars
into the spikes of the cactus fence.
The story is our escort;
without it we are blind."
When we are baptized
we are baptized into a story,
a story of God's loving acts,
a story of relationship,
a trinity of relationship.
The story is our escort
out of the little circle of our self
into the arms of the Church
sheltered under the wings of God.
Do you begin to see that
this whole article of the Creed
is about connectedness?
about community?
about relationship?
The story into which

we are baptized
keeps us from blundering
through life thinking
we are alone, abandoned,
on our own.
Thinking we are more important than.
Thinking we are less important than.
For we are held
under the boughs
of a sheltering
family tree.

V. We look for the resurrection of the dead

The author Susan Palo Cherwien
relates this memory:
When I was a little girl
in northeastern Ohio,
I used to dread saying
my night-time prayer
"Now I lay me down to sleep . . . "
because of *that* phrase
"If I should die before I wake . . . "
I felt that saying such words
out loud
was just *inviting trouble*
into my dark room.
and I scrunched my eyes tight shut
wishing away
whatever I might have
conjured into my dark room,
until I fell asleep.
But by the time
I was in high school
and singing in a community chorus
performing Handel's *Messiah,*
something had changed
something in me had changed.
Because when I heard the bass soloist
begin to sing that lovely recitative
haloed by strings

"Behold, I tell you a mystery:
we shall not all sleep,
but we shall all be changed..."
I knew in my heart
that those words were true
and I no longer
had to scrunch my eyes shut
at the thought of death.
What changed me?
The Holy Spirit pressuring me
from within
to evolve,
to change, to become more,
to become a person willing
to risk, to love, to be vulnerable.
The story changed me, the Word of God,
the poetry of hymns sung over and over,
the Spirit of God
working through
the story, the song
to bring refreshing rain, water, wisdom,
and joy.

VI. and the life of the world to come

The Spirit,
the Giver of Life,
prods us,
provokes us
pressures us from within
to become
to become more
to become Christs
in this world
now.
here.
—to become , like Christ, so sure
of our shelter under the wings of God
that we can risk
becoming vulnerable,
taking down our walls
—to become, like Christ, so in love
with the creation God has made,
and all its people
that we can hear
the silent sigh of the suffering
and sorrowful
and reach out without
thought of self-interest
—to become, like Christ, so infused with God
that God's intent and desire
are done through us
regardless of the consequences.

Our prayers to the Holy Spirit
are to change us,
to warm us,
to water us
so that the earth
this earth
may become a garden
and all of us
becoming trees bearing much fruit:
fruit of compassion, fruit of mercy, of joy,
fruit of laughter, dancing, delight,
fruit of justice,
fruit of peace.

VII. Amen

Amen. So be it. Amen.
Or, as Captain Picard would say,
"Make it so."
Amen is a response.
In the Jewish tradition
if you pronounce a blessing
by yourself
you do not say "Amen."
But if you hear someone else
pronounce a blessing,
you are to respond "Amen."
Do you begin to see
that even the word
"Amen"
is about community
about connectedness
about Trinity
about relationship?
About the Spirit
prodding us
pressuring us
provoking us
to evolve
to change
to become more?
pressuring us
to a transformed life?

And so we say, "Amen"
to God as the Creator.
We say "Amen"
to God as the Christ.
We say "Amen"
to God as the Holy Spirit—
with all of creation
and all of its creatures
of every species and kind—
from age to age
eternally.
Amen.

THAT WE MAY BE ONE

I. The Road to Emmaus

Jesus, the Health of the World,
enlighten our minds…

Our bodies are our teachers
Our bodies mediate all we know of the world
Everything we think we know
comes to us through our five senses—
hearing, touch, taste, smell, sight.
Our brains and our skin
Develop from the same primal tissue
Our guts have more neurons
than our spinal cords
Our whole bodies think
Our whole bodies remember
Our bodies are our teachers.
And so the gospel writer Luke
tells us the story of the two disciples
encountering the Risen Christ
on the road to Emmaus:

they hear him—
        asking questions
        interpreting the scriptures
they hear him
        for most of the seven miles to Emmaus
and do not recognize the Christ
until they break bread
        they touch
        they smell
        they taste
and finally, they see.

II. Our Hearts Burn within Us

Jesus walks with us, Ever awaiting
Our invitation, Stay, do not part.

A wisdom story:

The teacher asked the disciples:
Can any of you give me an example
of enlightenment or holiness?

One disciple stood and told the following story:
I heard about a saint in the area
who, wanting to visit a dying friend,
and fearing to travel by night,
said to the sun,
"In the name of God
stay on in the sky
till I reach the village
where my friend is dying."
And the sun stopped dead in the sky
Till the holy one reached the village.

The teacher thought awhile and replied:
Would it not have been better
for the holy person
to overcome his fear
of travelling by night?

III. The Good Shepherd

In her book
The Solace of Open Spaces
Gretel Ehrlich
tells her stories
of leaving academia
on the east coast
and becoming
a sheep-herder
in Wyoming
her isolation
her solitude
her responsibility
to the sheep
And she relates
that the sheep-herder
often leads the sheep
from behind
out of sight of the flock
prodding
urging
suggesting
the sheep-herder's task
is to get the sheep
from waterhole to waterhole
from used-up pasture to abundant pasture
to urge them forward
toward what they need to live
toward what they need
to grow

IV. That Thursday Night

Jesus, the Health of the world,
enlighten our minds, great Redeemer.

It is at the core of the sun
that photons, light particles
are produced by the fusion reaction.
And the newly formed photons
have to journey through
the plasma layer from the core.
They bounce and ricochet,
they detour and backtrack,
making their way to the sun's surface—
a journey that takes 100,000 years.

From the sun's inner layer to its surface,
the journey takes a week.
From the sun's surface to earth,
nine minutes.

That Thursday night,
the night before Jesus' death,
Jesus broke bread with the disciples
they heard, they touched, smelled, tasted
helping their bodies remember.

That Thursday night,
Jesus prayed that all his followers may be one.
But it has now been 2,000 years
we have bounced and ricocheted
we have detoured and backtracked
we are still making the journey to oneness
oneness in Christ.
Are our hearts burning
within us?

V. That They May Be One

Did you know that
photons seem to be communicating
with each other as they move
through space?
Did you know that
the hemoglobin in our blood
is only one element different
than the chlorophyll
in plants?
Did you know that
rats will struggle to free
a caged rat and
celebrate together
when they succeed?
Did you know that
the sun sings
while it fires light for our earth?
Did you know that
humpback whales
work as a finely-tuned team
to catch herring?
Did you know that the oxygen
that our brains need to think
is a gift of the plants?
Did you know that
after 9/11, a Maasai tribe in Kenya
blessed fourteen cows
and gave them to the people of the United States
as a gift of compassion?

There are so many connections
in the world
if we open our eyes
if we let our hearts burn within us
There are so many layers
of connectedness
that we are being prodded to see
toward which we are being prodded
    the photons are chatting
    the sun is singing
    the rats are celebrating
    the whales are dining
    the Maasai are blessing.
Our bodies will teach us
our bodies will understand for us.
one bread
one cup
we hear
we touch
we smell
we taste
and finally,
we see.
And Christ stands
in the midst
of us all.

VI. The High Priestly Prayer

There is really
no exact verb "to be" in ancient Hebrew—
all the language of God in Hebrew scripture
is more about God doing
about God's activity—
Psalm 23, for example,
being more accurately translated
"God shepherds me"
than "God is my shepherd"
and God's pronouncement to Moses
more accurately
"I will be there howsoever I will be there"
I will be there howsoever I will be there
is God's answer
when Moses
asks for God's name
after seeing the burning bush
I will be there howsoever I will be there.
And in the great prayer
that the writer John
recounts from
That Thursday night,
Jesus places himself in that
I will be there howsoever I will be there:
"I in them and You in me,
That they may be completely one."

Christ in us
and God in Christ
I will be there howsoever I will be there
in us.
And how shall this connectedness be known?
By doing,
by activity
by loving
"so that the love with which
you have loved me
may be in them."
I will be there howsoever I will be there.

VII. Christ Ascending on High

French paleontologist and priest
Teilhard de Chardin
wrote:
"Because, O Christ, you have
descended into hell
and ascended into heaven,
you so fill all creation
that it is blessedly impossible
to escape you."
Christ is incarnate: Heaven is in earth
Christ ascended: Earth is in Heaven
Heaven and earth are intertwined.
The holy is among us
Christ is among us
walking with us on the road
waiting to be recognized

A Gaelic rune:
I saw stranger yestere'en,
I put food in the eating place,
drink in the drinking place
music in the listening place.
And in the sacred name of the Triune
he blessed myself and my house
my cattle and my dear ones.
And the lark said in her song,
often goes the Christ in the stranger's guise.
Bless.

Prayer

O God,
O I will be there howsoever I will be there,
God of all nations, all creation,
Blessed are you,
for there is nowhere we can flee from your presence;
Blessed are you,
for you have woven creation
out of your holy love;
you have breathed your life
into all people;
your oceans are in our tears;
your name pulses in our heartbeat.
In Christ,
Holy Love has been made flesh
and dwelt among us.
So draw us into your very heart,
that we may be your loving hands in this world,
the saving word,
the compassionate voice.
So draw us into you
that our differences
fade into blessings,
our unity deeper than life itself.
Amen

SONGS OF THE SPIRIT

I. This-ness

In the fourteenth century
John Duns Scotus wrote
that God did not create
genus and species
but that God created
Haecceitas
or "this-ness"
From the book of Genesis:
"At the beginning of God's creating
of the heavens and the earth,
when the earth was wild and waste,
rushing-spirit of God hovering over the face of the waters—God spoke"...
Haecceity
"This-ness"
At the beginning of God's creating,
rushing-spirit of God
was already hovering
already flitting
already exploring
already protecting
The Here
the Now, the plethora of all things
is the sphere of the Spirit's activity
creation—
all 14 billion years of it.

If you have ever seen
the opening of the TV show *The Big Bang Theory,*
you have seen the flashing slides of history
speeding by
(—And here's a good dinner party trivia question:
how many are there?
109.)
But the first slide in this flashing historical tour
is a slide of mitosis,
the division of living cells
that probably first occurred
at about 2.5 billion years ago,
so roughly 12 billion years
are missing
years in which the Spirit of God
was hovering over the waters.
"This-ness"
haecceity
began long before living cells,
long before mammals,
long before humans—
the sphere of the Spirit
is all of creation
the sphere of the Spirit is "This-ness"

II. Matter and Spirit

The rushing Spirit of God
hovers over "this-ness"
flitting
protecting
exploring
prodding
Jesuit paleontologist
Teilhard de Chardin insisted that
There is no matter
without spirit.
This has grave implications
for our attitudes
for our behavior
There is no matter without spirit.
Maples and dogwood
have spirit
Atom and quark
have spirit
these fingers
these stones
these voices
that wind
that sun
those rivers
If we have eyes to see
if we have ears to hear.

Elizabeth Barrett Browning wrote
in her long poem *Aurora Leigh*:
"Earth's crammed with heaven.
And every common bush afire with God.
But only he who sees takes off his shoes . . ."
One of the most valuable attitudes
that we can cultivate
is the state of wonder.
We should be astonished
that hearts beat
that monarch butterflies find their way back
to a home they've never seen
that tides ebb and flow.
Teilhard wrote:
"Nothing here below is profane
for those who have eyes to see."
The Spirit of God is coursing through
everything that is
hovering
blessing
opening our eyes
to wonder.

III. Wildfire

When we chant
Veni Creator Spiritus
when we sing
"Come, Holy Spirit, Come"
we are not praying
a charming little lamplight
into our lives
what will come
is power
what will come is fire
not a neat little confined candle flame
in this neat little corner
of our lives
but a Fort McMurray wildfire
that changes everything it touches
with the fire of Love.
When we chant the Spirit
into our lives
we are praying into ourselves
the wildfire of indiscriminate love
we will find ourselves
prodded
to no abstract love of
neighbor
but to actively working for their thriving
for their welfare,
to stop by the roadside
for those different from us.

We do not pray the Spirit into our lives and declare,
"Only in this corner,
only these people,
only my church."
The Spirit comes like wildfire,
when we open the door, when we say "come,"
filling all the dark places
all the fear places,
with wildly indiscriminate Love.

A story from the desert Fathers:

Abba Lot came to Abba Joseph and said: Father, according as I am able, I keep my little rule, and my little fast, my prayer, meditation and contemplative silence; and, according as I am able, I strive to cleanse my heart of thoughts: now what more should I do? The elder rose up in reply and stretched out his hands to heaven, and his fingers became like ten lamps of fire. He said: Why not become fire?

IV. Rose Petals

In mediæval churches
there was often,
in the ceiling of the crossing,
or the dome,
what was called
the "Holy Ghost hole"
and through that hole
on the festival of Pentecost,
a dove would be released
above the gathered people,
to remind them of the Spirit hovering over creation,
hovering in the form of a dove
at Jesus' baptism,
and red rose petals
would be showered down
on the gathered people
to remind them
of the tongues of flame
on the heads of all
on that Shavuot gathering
fifty days after the resurrection.
Rose petals drifting down,
the dove hovering
above the people.
Not just for the disciples,
but for all the people.

Not just for clergy, or scholars, or mystics, or monks—
the dove hovers above all creation
over all "this-ness."
The rose petals of fire
alight on all who open the door
and pray "Come."
The Holy Spirit of God connects our being
to every other aspect of Being
Like the Higgs field, like quantum entanglement,
like the branches to the vine,
like the web of existence.
In the wild and indiscriminate Love
of the Spirit of God,
there is no isolated being
no isolated act.
The rose petals drift down on all.
Come Holy Spirit,
and spread Thy Goldenwings in us.

V. Living in the Spirit

Etty Hillesum,
who died in Auschwitz,
wrote in her diary:
"All disasters stem from us.
Why is there a war?
...Because I and my neighbor
and everyone else
do not have enough love."
To live in the Spirit
is to live in the quantum field
of love that "surpasses all understanding."
To live in the Spirit
is to love, care and serve
with wild unbounded love
without limits,
without stipulations.
In the Sermon on the Mount
Jesus made it clear
that it is not just our actions
that matter
but the motivations of the heart
behind the actions.
Nothing in this universe
disappears without a trace

Charitable acts motivated by
the need to be the center of attention
make the universe vibrate
with the energy of self-centeredness
Emotion, intent, are energy.
Nothing disappears without a trace.
What are we sending out into the universe?
Joy?
Nobility?
Truth?
Beauty?
Love without need for return?
Nothing disappears without a trace.

VI. Light Cones

In a 2016 article in the *New York Times,*
science writer Dennis Overbye
described
Einstein's theory of relativity
and its relation to time.
We each live in a present moment
that is slightly different
from everyone else's present moment.
Everywhere we look beyond Now
is already the past
and even a glance at our neighbor
shows us our neighbor's face
a nanosecond ago,
the time it took for the light
to reach our eyes.
So we all have a partial view of the universe,
called a "light cone"
and we need each other to see the whole picture
to get a more complete view of "this-ness"
We need what our ancestors saw,
who tried to show us in chant and icon and poem
we need what the artists see
what the farmers see
what the children see
what the scientists see
to begin to understand the universe
and our place.

Catholic theologian Karl Rahner wrote that
The Holy Spirit
is always pressuring us from within
to evolve.
But we cannot evolve alone.
we need what others see, and we cannot
we need what the past saw and we forgot
The world is turning
and the Spirit is pressuring us
to evolve.
For the world to evolve
we need to evolve
into living flames of creative fire
drawing from each other
drawing from the One Creative Flame
underlying all that is.

VII. Spirit-verbs: Becoming

When we open ourselves
to the Spirit of God,
the Spirit of Life,
we open the door
to see outside and beyond
our own little "Light cone"
of the Present moment.
By singing, "Come,"
By chanting, "Come,"
By praying "Come,"
we open the door to move from
Being to
Becoming.
Look at all the hymns to the Holy Spirit—
they are all Verbs!
When we speak of God, we often use
Nouns: Creator, Sustainer, Shepherd, Rock.
When we speak of Christ, we often use
Adjectives: loving, compassionate, merciful, just.
When we speak of the Spirit we use
Verbs: seeking, hovering, pleading, igniting
We sing: Come, seek, kindle,
Fall, break, melt, mold, fill;
Come, bestow,
Cleanse, quench, cure, correct.

We call on the Spirit of God
when our desire is to
move from Being
to Becoming
when we are ready
to evolve,
to see the world with wider view.
The universe needs
every precious,
unique human being
to evolve,
to become,
to become what we were meant to be.

VIII. From Wonder to Peace

The Spirit of God
ignites in us Wonder
And wonder moves us to
Gratitude.
According to the Babylonian Talmud,
the pious Jew
is to bless God
100 times each day—
"Blessed are you. O God
for voices, for pipes for flute
for beauty for tulips for spring"
Wonder moves us to
Gratitude
and Gratitude moves us to
Compassion
for we cannot negate or revile
that for which we have given thanks
Compassion is a deep suffering-with
The Hebrew word for compassion,
rachamim
means to feel in the womb—
to feel deep in the inmost parts of our body—
the suffering of others

Compassion leads us to Justice
And Justice will lead us to
Peace.
The Spirit of God is still
hovering over creation,
over haecceity,
over "This-ness"
over all things, all people
pressuring us to evolve
to become fire
to burst into flames of
indiscriminate Love
wild creativity.
The universe needs us to evolve.
And so, let us pray,
"Come, Holy Spirit."

THE CHURCH REFORMING

I. A New Thing

"Behold,
I am doing a new thing,"
declares God.
"Do you not see it?"

A new thing.
unexpected
the universe spirals
toward diversity
toward complexity
newness.
Surprising us
with smaller and smaller subatomic particles
astonishing us
with larger and larger galaxies
serenading us
with deep songs from the nebulas
and stars.
Unexpected
wonder full.
God at work in the universe
mysterious.

Beneath the midnight galaxies
surrounded by clusters
of angel song—
A new thing.
Unexpected.
God and human
come together
in the chamber
of the heart—
heart of human
heart of God
unexpected.
a new thing.

II. Stepping Beyond

"Let the same mind
be in you
that was in Christ Jesus,
who, though he was
in the form of God...
emptied himself,
taking the form of a slave."

The Greek word
for repentance
metanoia
means
"go beyond
the mind
that you have."
Jesus walked the limestone roads
of Galilee
calling the people
to step beyond.
To step beyond fear
to step beyond grasping for power
to step beyond who's in and who's out
to step beyond self-loathing.
Samuel Torvend writes:
"Reform was at
the very heart
of Jesus' own
public work..."

calling for reform
in the daily lives
of pious and observant people
calling for reform
of and oppressive
and punitive
understand of God.
Go beyond the mind that you have—
"Let this mind be in you"—
Christ healed
Christ fed
Christ taught
Christ loved,
and—
Fear Not—
Christ lives.

III. Becoming a New Creation

"And the One who was seated
on the throne said,
"See, I am making
all things new."

The journey
in Christ
is a journey of
becoming,
of
new creation.
The heart of God
enters the
human heart and—
new creation
the mind of Christ
opens the
human mind and—
new creation
(Behold, I make all things new)

The Spirit of God
joins new heart and new mind
in the human body and—
sparks burst forth
fire flames upward:
wonder
gratitude
compassion
justice
peace
new creation
in this body
in this life
in this place

IV. New Every Morning

"The steadfast love of God
never ceases;
God's mercies never come
to an end;
they are new every morning."

God is always
drawing the universe
toward newness
God is ever
beckoning us
to become
to become new creations
to step beyond.
Wonders surround us
Can we remain unmoved?
Shall we stare uncomprehending,
as Luther says,
"like a cow
staring at a new gate?"
The universe spirals
toward diversity
toward complexity

Wake, awake
it sings in the ear,
Step beyond,
become new
become the person
God created you to be:
prophets, apostles, white-robed martyrs,
teachers, carpenters, physicists, poets
unexpected.
mysterious.
In the heart of God
In the mind of Christ
In the fire of the Spirit.

SING THE NEW SONG

I. Getting to Singing

Bernice Johnson Reagon
one of the founders of
the vocal group Sweet Honey in the Rock
said in an interview with Bill Moyers:
"Songs are a way
to get to singing.
The singing is what
you're aiming for.
You cannot sing a song
and not change
your condition."
Behold, I make all things new, says God.
Our brains have evolved
to remember negative experiences
more than positive experiences
probably to help us survive
over the millennia
(no! don't eat that berry! remember?!)
it is said
that our brains are velcro
for bad memories
and teflon
for good memories
but—to keep
the positive effect
of a good experience
to make it a lasting part
of our human values
and life experience
we have to hold it
in our thoughts
for at least 20 seconds

allowing it to find
a permanent niche
in our thoughts
allowing it to shape
who we are
Imagine
what happens
when a group of 100 people
is singing a hymn together
a hymn about
the glory of creation
the lovingkindness of God
the life of Christ
a hymn
about the nobility
built into humans
by a loving God
imagine how that thought
gets planted deeply
indelibly
as we sing
and sing together
shaping us
forming us
changing us
Songs are a way
to get to singing…
You cannot sing
and not change
your condition.

II. Singing Story

Have you not seen?
Have you not heard?
Has it not been
told to you from the beginning?
God is the Everlasting God
the Creator
of the ends
of the earth.
So begins our story—
with the Everlasting God.
From God speaking the Light
into being
up to today's dawning
we are all part
of a grand story.
And we all have chapters to add
to the story
and we all have chants
and descants
to layer on the story
Human beings
survive and grow
by stories
we are woven
into community
by stories.

When we talk during the
daylight hours
to each other
we talk about
money, health,
problems
But when the sun sets,
and we sit in the darkness,
human conversation
naturally
moves to stories.
As followers of Christ
as beloved ones of God
we gather
we light candles
and we sing stories
all part of the one great story
the story
of a generous and self-giving God
opening wide
the gate of Heaven.

III. Transforming Love

Benedictine Joan Chittister wrote that,
like God, like Christ,
we are called in our lives to cultivate
a cosmic heart.
"Create in me
a clean heart, O God,"
we sing in Psalm 51.
A clean heart.
The heart is the place
where the whole person
comes together—
body, mind, spirit
What is intended
in the mind
takes up residence
in the body
and the spirit
What is done
in the body
takes residence
in the spirit
and the mind
All are interwoven
The heart is where
change takes place
where transformation
happens

As St. Makarios the Egyptian wrote:
"The heart
is a small vessel;
and yet dragons
and lions are there,
and there poisonous creatures
and all the treasures
of wickedness;
rough uneven paths
are there,
and gaping chasms.
There likewise is God,
there are angels,
the heavenly cities
and the treasuries
of grace,
all things are there."
Create in me
a clean heart,
O God.

IV. Visible Love

A fourteenth century ceiling fresco
in the Chora Church in Istanbul
depicts the angel of God
rolling up the heavens
like a scroll
at the end of time.
And it truly would be the end of time
were the sun to be rolled up
and placed in the scriptorium,
for every living thing
depends on the sun.
Whenever we eat,
we are eating sunlight
When we think,
our brains are fueled
by the oxygen released by plants
reacting to sunlight.
Loren Eiseley spoke well
when he said,
Consciouness "burns
by the power of the leaf."
The fire of the sun
resides in every living thing.
Hildegard von Bingen wrote
"God has arranged
everything in the universe
in consideration
of everything else."

All emerges from God
all is sustained by God
visible love
from the Heart of Love.
Who are we then
not to participate in that
outpouring of Love?
Who are we then
not to live out each moment
of each day
immersed in
and pouring out
that loving connection
to all things?
Romans 1, verse 20:
"For since the creation of the world
God's invisible qualities—
God's eternal power
and divine nature—
have been seen
through the things
God has made."
Visible Love
from Invisible
divine Love.

V. The Heart of God

We become what we sing
What we consciously
participate in
becomes incarnate
in us
We should be as careful of the words
that we sing
as we are
of the food
that we put into
our body
Singing together
is a powerful
life-changing act
"You cannot
sing a song
and not change
your condition"
By singing together
of God's love
we are drawn more and more
into an awareness
of the cosmic Heart
of God

By singing of the
Spirit's fire
we become
more and more open
to the Spirit
creating a new heart
in us
By singing of the
beauty of creation
we shape our lives
as part of a great story
and community

Have you not heard?
Have you not known?
Our lives lived
in the heart of God
are lives of Communion
of Compassion
of Becoming
of Story and
Song.

THROUGH THE CHURCH THE SONG GOES ON

I. Flight of the Dove

In the Middle Ages—
centuries before Martin Luther—
on the Feast of Pentecost
the choir would chant
what was called
a sequence hymn
Veni Sancte Spiritus
"Come Holy Ghost"
and the congregation
would then respond
by singing
in the vernacular
in German
a single stanza
Nun bitten wir
—Now to the Holy Spirit
let us pray—
and at the singing
a live dove
would be released
into the sanctuary
flying
weaving
soaring
between the people
over the people
among them

Nun bitten wir—
connecting ancient chant—
pentatonic
based on a five-note scale—
connecting chant
with folk song
Latin with German
lofty thought
with earthly flight.
And so today
in the church
from a commissioned
twentieth century hymn
to the ancient texts of Fortunatus
the church sings
still accompanied by the soaring flight
of the spirit.

II. Our Ancestor Song

Martin Luther
added three stanzas
to *Nun bitten wir*
and his collaborator
Johann Walther
published it in 1525.
Here it is in our hands
roughly 500 years later
a link to our story
a link to our ancestors
We do not journey alone.
One hundred years after Luther
the pastor-poet
Paul Gerhardt
collaborated
with his friend and
colleague
Johann Crüger
at the Nikolaikirche
in central Berlin
to write an Easter hymn
bright with joy.

Auf, auf, mein Herz
"Awake my heart with Gladness."
Here it is in our hands
roughly 400 years later
a link to our story
a link to our ancestors
a link to God's story
We do not journey alone
And the Holy Spirit
swoops
and soars
in joy
around us.

III. The Dancing Hymn

Between the times
of Luther and Gerhardt
a gifted priest and composer
labored in Mantua, Italy
writing madrigals
and *balletti*
light hearted dancetunes
and love songs
And soon
after one collection by this Giovanni Gastoldi
was published
in 1591
it came into the hands
of hymnist Johann Lindemann
in Gotha, Germany,
who found this *balletto*
especially entrancing:
A lieta vita, Amor c'invita,
fa la la la la, fa la la.
Just seven years
after its first press
A lieta vita
became
In dir ist Freude
with *fa-la-las*
transformed into
alleluias.

Two hundred and fifty years pass
and in England
Catherine Winkworth
encounters *In dir ist Freude*
and translates
it into English verse
published in 1858.
Italian high art melody
German hymnic poetry
British translation
and still the hymn dances
in the church.

IV. Fortunatus and Neale

If there is ever
an Indiana Jones type
adventurer
interested in hymnody
(strangers things have happened . . .)
I would commission
that person to find
Venantius Fortunatus'
last volume:
Hymns For All the Festivals of the Christian Year.
This sixth century poet
who wrote
"Sing My Tongue the Glorious Battle"
"The Royal Banners Forward Go" and
"Hail Thee Festival Day"
wrote a hymn for *every festival*
in the church year—
and they are
lost
lost,
lost!
Across France to Poitiers,
across the Alps
to the mosaic tombs of Ravenna,
west to the archives of Milan
a great adventure
waiting to happen!

The Oxford movement
in England in the mid-1800s
which called for a
return to the Church's
more ancient Catholic roots
spurred John Mason Neale
to creatively and lovingly translate
into nineteenth century English verse
the rich Latin images of this sixth century poet
          "Faithful cross, true sign of triumph,
          be for all the noblest tree;
          none in foliage, none in blossom
          none in fruit your equal be."
In the twentieth century
To John Mason Neale's text
Lutheran Carl Schalk composes a new melody.
How impoverished we would be
without these finely-crafted words!
How blessed we are,
How blessed to sing!

V. The Poet's Vision

Our concerns in life fluctuate
our concerns in the church change
we oscillate between
times of abundance and
times of drought
days of certainty and
days of doubt
between being oppressor and oppressed
between hale and ill
between peace and war
and always
always
we need the poet's vision
to put into words
what we need to express
to put into sound
what we may have forgotten
or misunderstood
or mislaid
we need the composer's talent
to put the words
into our voices
as communal song
as the Church's song

These are words
for community
for the times of abundance
and the times of drought
Truths we need to sing
to sing together
finely crafted
in the best words
and music of our time.

VI. Hymns Forming People

The previous hymn
was written in our time
by two Americans,
Richard Leach and Thomas Pavlechko.
people of this place
as is the hymn that follows.
Even more specifically
the hymn that follows
was written first
to be sung
within the walls of
Westwood Lutheran Church,
Saint Louis Park, Minnesota,
where Ronald Nelson had led the choirs
"O grant us, Christ, a deep humility"
a text for the church's anniversary
that took the shape of a servant hymn
as the words took the lead
as the words shaped themselves.
Words have life
words have power
they shape us
they form our faith
they transform
and form us into a people

they remind us of our story as a people
the grand drama
unfolding in our lives
and the life of the universe.
The hymns we sing
help us remember
whose, we are
to what we are called
how much we are loved
how much we are needed.

VII. The Spirit Hovers over the World

Latin hymns
German *Leisen*
German Chorales
Luther
Gerhardt
English translators
Neale
Winkworth
American hymns
Pavlechko
Leach
Nelson
But there is a great world
out there
a grand sphere
under the sway of Christ
and poets
in Spanish
and Swahili
and Mandarin
finely craft words
to remind us whose we are
composers
finely craft tunes
for community
to shape us into the body
of Christ
In the Philippines
Catholic and Anglican
come together
and again
bring us an
image:
wings.

The Spirit hovers
over the Pacific Ocean
over the Indian Ocean
over the Great Lakes
weaving
soaring
swooping
above and
around us.
Wings of Spirit
wings of fire
wings of peace

Prayer

Almighty and everliving God,
you fulfilled the promise of Easter
by sending the gift of the Holy Spirit.
Look upon your people
gathered in prayer,
open to receive the Spirit's flame.
May it come to rest in our hearts
and heal the divisions of word and tongue,
that with one voice
and one song
we may praise your name
in joy and thanksgiving;
through Jesus Christ, our Lord,
who lives and reigns with you
and the Holy Spirit,
one God,
now and forever.
Amen.

HOLY SPIRIT, LUMINOUS LIFE

Holy Spirit, living and life-giving
moving all that lives,
you are the root of all creation.
You wash all things clean,
scrubbing away their mistakes, their guilt,
anointing and healing their wounds.
You are life,
luminous, shining with praise,
renewing and reviving all.

(*De Spiritu Sancto*, Hildegard von Bingen)

I. Holy Spirit, Living and Life-giving

"At the beginning of God's creating
of the heavens and the earth
when the earth was wild and waste
darkness over the face of Ocean,
rushing-spirit of God
hovering over the face of the waters..."
Rushing-spirit of God
Hovering
from the beginning
Hovering like an eagle
protecting its young...

Hildegard von Bingen of the twelfth century
saw the Trinity in this way:
"The Father is brightness
and this brightness has a flashing forth
and in this flashing forth is fire
and these three are one."
For Hildegard,
the Holy Spirit, that fire,
ties everything in the universe together
like a bundle
all things connected
all things related
through the fire and breath of the Spirit.
About a century after Hildegard
John Duns Scotus wrote that
God's first idea was to pour out
divine infinite love
into finite, visible forms.

For Hildegard and for Duns Scotus,
love, divine love
is the underlying
invisible form of
all created things
Woven together by the fire of the Spirit
Taking shape by the creative Word
Sustained by the breath of God.

II. moving all that lives, you are the root of all creation

So—let's begin with wonder
wonder
that anything exists at all
wonder
that human hands play Bach, paint horizons, knead bread
wonder
that the surface of the Sun sings with over 100,000 tones
that dung beetles navigate by the Milky Way
that rats will pass by chocolate to free another rat trapped
    in a cage—and celebrate together afterward
wonder
that plants follow the sun
that the hemoglobin in our blood is just one element different
    from chlorophyll
wonder
that photons communicate with each other
wonder
We should take our thuribles
light hot the coals
sprinkle on the resin
of the *boswellia* plant
and step outside

incense the sun
        Holy are you
incense the dogwoods
        Holy are you
incense the wind
        Holy are you
incense Lake Michigan
        Holy are you
incense the dung beetles
        Holy are you
incense the starlit heavens
        Holy are you
Let us begin with wonder.
Gratitude will follow.

III. You wash all things clean

At the close of the rituals
of Yom Kippur
the Jewish Day of Atonement
after the fasting
after the sending out of the scapegoat into the desert
the High Priest offered
from the platform in front of the Temple
a final prayer.
And that prayer was?
a prayer for rain.
A prayer for rain?
After all the sounding of shofars
and *teshuvah*, repentance,
after the reconciliation,
after all this,
a prayer for rain?
But think.
Think how much benevolent human relationships
and being able to care about something beyond survival
depend upon the timely coming of rain.
The uprising and civil war in Syria began
after a five-year drought
what little food farmers could produce
in that arid region
dried up

Drought in China
and brushfires in Russia
limited the wheat that could be exported
to the dry Middle East
people hungered
farmers moved their extended families into the cities
stressing the resources,
the infrastructure
and neighbor began
to turn on neighbor
other humans became scapegoats
sent into the desert.
Ah, yes,
ah, yes,
let us indeed pray for rain
life-giving rain of earth
life-giving rain within the human heart.

IV. scrubbing away their mistakes, their guilt

In Ursula Le Guin's fantasy, *A Wizard of Earthsea,*
the Master Summoner warns
apprentice Ged
that one must carefully consider
the effects of one's decisions
because "to light a candle is to cast a shadow."
Even our actions intended for good
often have negative effects on
the Sky People, the Plant People, the Rock People,
the Winged People, the Finned People.
Biologists hybridize a short wheat
less susceptible to blowdown by heavy rain and wind
in hopes of feeding the world—
and create a grain whose multiple glutens make many people ill.
Biochemists alter a corn seed
to be less susceptible to damage from the corn borer—
and monarch and swallowtail butterflies
begin to disappear from the countryside.
Even with good intentions
we cast a shadow
And in our ignorance and pride and self-absorption
we cast even more.

On Good Friday
many of us sing or chant the Solemn Reproaches

Perhaps we need
to prayerfully and thoughtfully craft
sung reproaches on behalf of the earth:
"O my people, what more could I have done for you
that I have not done?
Answer me."
That which we have done
That which we have not done
That which we have done unintentionally
because we did not see
how the Holy Spirit
ignites and binds together
all things.
Reproaches
On behalf of the earth:
"Holy, holy, holy God,
Holy and Mighty,
Holy and Immortal,
have mercy on us."

V. anointing and healing their wounds

All that is needed
Is already here.
If we had eyes to see.

Hildegard von Bingen was also
a healer, an herbalist:
she wrote a book on medicine.
Victoria Sweet, a twenty-first century physician
at a hospital for those in poverty in San Francisco
was at a loss at how to relieve
her patients' unhealing bedsores
She turned to Hildegard's recipe for a poultice
using common herbs
and the bedsores healed.
All that is needed
is already here.
Baudelaire wrote that
"we walk through forests of things
that regard us with affectionate looks"
The Plant People, the Tree People
stand among us as relatives
regarding us with "affectionate looks"
offering gifts:
Oxygen from the photosynthesis of plants
makes consciousness possible.
Near poison ivy grows jewelweed
whose leaves relieve the itching and sores.

All that is needed
is already here
for the body
for the human spirit
The Holy Spirit hovers over creation
like an eagle protecting its young
The Resurrected Christ walks in the Garden
The divine Love of God is poured out
into all things.
All that is needed
is already here.
Newness
Healing
Hope
Have mercy, O God.
Open our eyes.

VI. You are life, luminous, shining with praise

Mitakuye oyasin
All my relations,
the Lakota say
about all beings
all creations
All my relations.
All the elements of our bodies
were formed from stars,
either exploding
or colliding.
We are cousins to the stars
We are cousins to the trilobites
first to be able to see the creation
500 million years ago
We are genetic cousins
to every living thing
cousins
to every created thing
All My Relations.

In the Sierra Nevada mountains
of Colombia
the Kogi people
tend terraces of healing plants
on the high slopes.
And while the workers
weed the terraces,
a priest stands in their midst
praying
that the plants
may feel no pain.

All my relations.
The Spirit moving through
all created things
the Christ holding all things
together
the divine Love of God
poured into visible forms.
We were all made for relationship
From the sun and the stars
to the quark and atom
to the trilobite and the Kogi.
All my relations.

VII. renewing and reviving all

Roman Catholic theologian Karl Rahner wrote that
the Holy Spirit is always
pressuring us from within
to evolve.
The Milky Way
is essentially
a two-armed spiral galaxy
which we see transversely,
in cross-section
on a clear night
Those arms are density waves
fields of becoming
where new stars are born.
A galaxy,
says physicist Brian Swimme
is not a thing, but rather,
"an activity."
Back in 1962,
Lutheran theologian Joseph Sittler wrote,
"We do not have a daring,
penetrating, life-affirming
Christology of nature…
[Humans] blasphemously
strut about this hurt and
threatened world as if they owned it…
The *telos* [goal] of doctrine
is action,
the fulfillment of right-teaching
is not right-teaching,
but decision and deed."

The Holy Spirit is pressuring
us from within to evolve,
to evolve into circumspect,
compassionate, wise vessels
of the Holy Spirit,
becoming,
becoming
becoming
like newborn stars.

VIII. The Spirit of Eight

and so—
an eighth reflection
seven for the days of creation
seven for the gifts of the Spirit
seven for the number of completion
seven would have been a goodly number
a good place to stop
but let's go to eight
the number of the new creation
the eighth day
the resurrection day
The Holy Spirit hovers over creation
like an eagle protecting its young
the Holy Spirit
calls gathers enlightens
pressures us from within
to evolve
the starlit heavens need us to do so
the glorious sun's life-giving ray
the whiteness of the moon at even
all need us to do so

And, so, let us pray:
Holy Spirit, living and life-giving
moving all that lives,
you are the root of all creation.
You wash all things clean,
scrubbing away their mistakes, their guilt,
anointing and healing their wounds.

You are life,
luminous, shining with praise,
renewing and reviving all—
to you be honor and praise forever,
who reigns with God and the Risen Christ
unto all ages of ages.
Amen

A sending from our sister Hildegard:
Be not lax in celebrating.
Be not lazy in the festive service of God.
Be ablaze with enthusiasm.
Let us be an alive, burning offering
before the altar of God!
Amen

TO GOD I GIVE MY MELODY

Martin Luther on God

"God is a supernatural,
inscrutable being
who exists at the same time
in every little seed,
whole and entire,
and yet also
in all
and above all
and outside all created things.
There is no need to enclose God here,
for a body is
much, much too wide
for the Godhead;
it could contain
many thousand Godheads.

On the other hand,
it is also far, far too narrow
to contain one Godhead.
Nothing is so small
but God is still smaller,
nothing so large
but God is still larger…
nothing is so broad
but God is still broader,
nothing so narrow,
but God is still narrower.
God is an inexpressible being,
above and beyond
all that can be described
or imagined."

"Confession Concerning Christ's Supper," 1528

I. Steeped in the Church Fathers

Many people who grew up Lutheran,
if they were to
do a family history project,
might discover
that as far back as they can research,
their ancestors
were Lutheran,
especially if the ancestors
stem from
Germany or
Nordic countries.
And if not raised Lutheran
very likely
most were taught by
or preached to
or confirmed by
someone who had
a long history in
this branch of Christianity.
So what gets passed on in Lutheran communities
is roughly fifteen generations
of unspoken attitude
about Martin Luther
vibrating in bones
shaping our attitudes and ideas.

And so in such communities
there is a sort of *it goes without saying*
mythology around Luther
as if he were just plunked down on earth
in the end of the fifteenth century
separate from all that preceded him.
But he was a person—
a German Roman Catholic
shaped by the ideas of his time
and of those who came before him
just as we are shaped by our time
and all who have come before us—
whether we choose to acknowledge it
or not.
He was schooled in the classics:
the *trivium*—grammar, logic, rhetoric—the basics,
from which we get the word trivial—
and the *quadrivium*—arithmetic, geometry, music, astronomy.
He studied Greek and Latin, philosophy and theology.

(cont.)

As an Augustinian monk,
he studied those we call the church fathers
and in his writings, he quoted them often,
mostly favorably—except Jerome and Origen!—
from Irenaeus to John Duns Scotus.
And, among his favorites—Bernard of Clairvaux and Bonaventure,
Augustine and Ambrose of Milan.
So when Martin Luther began translating
hymns from the Latin into German
so that they could be sung in German
by the average church-goer—
among those he chose was
Veni redemptor gentium by Ambrose
which he translated as
Nun komm der Heiden Heiland
and we sing in a double translation
from Ambrose's Latin into Luther's German into English
    by William Reynolds:
Savior of the Nations Come.
John Mason Neale
made a translation directly from
Latin into English
Come Thou Redeemer of the Earth

but it is the translation from Luther's German
that has stayed with us—
giving us a perspective on the coming of Christ across time—
from the fourth century through the sixteenth century
and the nineteenth century
linking us back through the centuries
of Christ's church,
by the gift
of translation.

II. Classical Latin Poetry

Not only the church fathers influenced Luther
but also classical Latin poetry.
The composer Johann Walter
after hearing "Isaiah in a vision did of old"
asked Luther how he came to have
such good instruction
in the versification of texts.
Walter reports:
"…whereupon the good man
laughed at my simplicity and said:
'I learned this from Virgil,
who has the power so artfully
to adapt his verses and his words
to the story he is telling…'"
Virgil, Horace
Hesiod, Ovid, Pindar—
from all of these Luther quotes
and from them he learned.
Now, German hymns really did exist
and were sung before Luther,
but most singing in liturgy
was by the choir.
Wanting a solid Christmas hymn in German
Luther chose the Middle German
Ghelouet sistu Jhesu Crist
from at least the 1300s,
which he used as a first verse,
then crafted a seven stanza hymn
versifying the essence
of the prologue to John's Gospel:

"In the beginning was the Word..."
Using his *trivium* rhetorical toolbox,
Luther created a hymn in chiastic form—
chiasmus meaning "crossing"—
a form where the ideas double back on themselves
and cross in the center.
So, in the original seven verses,
the word "joy" predominates in stanzas 1 and 7,
the word "poor" in 2 and 6,
the word "world" in 3 and 5,
all coming to rest in the center,
the repeated word *Licht*, light,
in the central stanza—4.
The cross at the center, surrounded by Light,
the Light of Christ
entering the poor world,
bringing joy.

III. Aesop and Story

Luther was a lover of stories
and a story-teller
and next to the Bible
he said the best book
for living was...
Aesop's Fables.
"To say nothing about other books,
how could one prepare a finer book
on worldly heathen wisdom
than that ordinary, silly
children's book called Aesop."
Luther refers to Aesop's fables
over eighty times in his sermons
and commentaries
and in 1530 was preparing
his own translation with a preface.

Now—Katharina von Bora came into Luther's life
in 1525—she was 26, he was 41.
Their first child, Hans, was born in 1526,
followed by Elisabeth, Magdalena,
Martin, Paul, and Margarethe.
When the children were still little
Luther decided to write another Christmas hymn
based not on the eagle-winged
Prologue of John's Gospel,
but on a story—
the story of the angels
appearing to the shepherds
in the second chapter of Luke.

Perhaps some of the children sang the part of the angel
while others sang the shepherds' verses.
But it was story,
story sung, story taught, story learned—
story—
sung to a predominantly descending melody
of the Word coming to earth
and the angels coming
to sing and to proclaim.

IV. A Love of Song

Composer Johann Walter
further reported
how much Luther loved singing:
"he took great delight in music...
with whom I have passed
many a delightful hour in singing;
and often I have seen the dear man
wax so happy and merry in heart
over the singing that it was
well-nigh impossible to weary
or content him with it."
It was important to Luther
to translate into German and use in worship
the great canticles of the church,
along with the psalms and other chants.
He once had Walter and another musician, Rupff,
invited to Wittenberg
to advise him on selecting tones for chanting the lessons—
which in the mediæval lectionary
were the Epistle and Gospel.
Modes or tones had been assigned specific
moods or qualities
since the time of Plato.
"...he finally himself decided," Walter wrote,
"to appropriate the Eighth Tone to the Epistle,
since Paul was a very serious apostle,
and the Sixth Tone to the Gospel
saying:
'Our Christ is a good Friend,
and his words are full of love,
so we will take the Sixth Tone,
the tone of pleasant piety,
for the Gospel.'"

So Luther was concerned with not only
choosing the right words, but also the right notes.
Regarding translating, he wrote:
"To translate a Latin text and retain the Latin tone or notes …
doesn't sound polished or well-done.
Both the text and notes,
accents, melody and manner of rendering
ought to grow out of the Mother-tongue."
He instructed other translators
to use the simplest and most common words for hymns,
not for "Nurembergers,
but for coarse Saxons"
Not the language of "court or castle,"
but of the street.
And so we have from Luther's pen
a translation and versification
of the *Nunc dimittis,*
in short single syllable alliterative words,
Mit Fried
und Freud
ich fahr dahin.
The song of joy and peace
of Simeon
at the presentation of Jesus
in the temple.

V. Singing Theology

"It was a strange and deadly strife,
When death and life contended..."
Mors et vita duello
Conflixere mirando
Dux vitae mortuus
Regnat vivus...

Artist Lucas Cranach the Elder
was a colleague and friend
of the Luthers'
and in 1529
he painted a large panel
to open the eyes
of the people
to the theology
to which Luther's hymns
were opening people's
hearts.
The panel was titled "Law and Grace."
Divided into two panels
by a central tree,
the left panel depicts
Moses receiving the Ten Commandments
and a judging figure of Christ up in the clouds
being worshiped by angels.
The right panel is dominated
by the crucified Christ
trampling down death
and the risen Christ
aglow with new life,
Death has been defeated, trampled underfoot.

To portray this central message
in song
Luther used the eleventh century sequence
for Easter
Victimae paschali laudes,
and its related *Leise,*
Christ ist erstanden
as templates
for a hymn praising and proclaiming
the resurrected Christ:
Christ lag in Todesbanden.
In each stanza Luther used 7 lines—
7 being the number of wholeness,
of completeness,
the 7th line having 8 syllables—
8 the number of new creation,
new beginning
the number of sides
on early and mediæval baptismal fonts,
the 8th day, Sunday, Easter day,
newness,
springtime,
the Easter dawn.
Alleluia

VI. The Handmaid of God

Luther considered music
to be a gift of the Holy Spirit:
"I would certainly like to praise
music with all my heart
as the excellent gift of God
which it is and to commend it
to everyone...
from the beginning of the world
it has been instilled and implanted
in all creatures...
nothing is without sound or harmony...
Wondrous mysteries are here
suggested by the Spirit..."
"...Whether you wish to comfort the sad,
or terrify the happy, to encourage the despairing,
to humble the proud, to calm the passionate,
or to appease those full of hate,
what more effective means than music
could you find?
The Holy Spirit itself honors music
as an instrument of its proper work..."
he wrote.
Martin Luther played the lute,
he wrote motets,
his favorite composer was Josquin des Pres
he transcribed melodies from neumes,
he sang with his wife and children,
with his students and friends.

In 1538 he wrote
"A Preface for All Good Hymnals"
in poetic form
and has Lady Music speak.
Lady Music says:
"Of all the joys upon this earth
None has for mortals greater worth
Than what I give with my ringing
And with voices sweetly singing.
There cannot be an evil mood
Where there are singing folk so good...
But God in me more pleasure finds
Than in all joys of earthly minds...
To God I give my melody
And thanks in all eternity."

VII. Seeking Peace That the World Cannot Give

The early church fathers—Ambrose, Augustine, Bernard,
(well, but not Jerome
Luther said he had been done much harm by Jerome)
the classical Latin poets—Virgil, Horace
the early hymnwriters
the shapers of the Christian church
Aesop
the apostle Paul
the Hebrew scriptures—
(Luther was a professor of Old Testament)
all these were a part of the
genealogy of Martin Luther
the world of ideas
and wisdom
out of which he came
that shaped his ideas and attitudes
that vibrated in his cells and bones
that received new voice in his hymns
and melodies...
He was steeped in the classics
he was shaped by his education—parts of the *Small Catechism*
are reminiscent of
Cyril of Jerusalem's "Catechetical Lectures"—
He was troubled by
what he perceived to be
misunderstandings
misperceptions.
What he did not have was
peace of mind
peace of heart.
And the gift that he received
from the Holy Spirit
in studying the writings of
the apostle Paul,

especially the epistle to the Romans,
the gift he received
was a new sense that God is a
loving and merciful God, and that nothing
can destroy the compassion of God.
Each day Luther began
by signing himself
with the cross and saying,
"I am baptized into Christ"
No fear
no hurt
no war
no plague
no misdeed
no misperception
no misstep
can separate us from
God's constant love.
In the *Small Catechism*
Luther's suggests
that we begin each day
by making the sign of the cross
and saying
"I am baptized into Christ'
and trust that nothing
ultimately nothing
can separate us
from the love of God
in Christ.
(This is
most certainly
true.)

RISE, REMEMBER WELL THE FUTURE

...the Holy Spirit
calls,
gathers,
enlightens,
and sanctifies
the whole Christian church
and sustains it
with Jesus Christ
in the one common,
true faith...

Martin Luther, *The Small Catechism,* The Apostles' Creed, Third Article

I. Called/Gathered: "In the Beginning—Music"

II. Enlightened: "In the Beginning—Music, Word, Story"

III. Sanctified: "Holy, Holy, Holy—Here I Will Meet You"

IV. Sustained: S"Called to the Future, Which Is Christ"

I. Called/Gathered: "In the Beginning—Music"

Gregory of Nyssa wrote:
"The whole cosmos is a kind of
musical harmony whose musician
is God."
In the beginning
God, Immortal Love,
sang out into chaos,
"Light!"
And light answered the call
with a burst
of white hot radiance.
And with that burst
a high *glissando* began
like ten thousand thousand
violins, sliding, cascading
down to violas, to cellos—
over the first mere 400,000 years—
to a double bass pedal tone
50 octaves below human hearing,
settling into a foundational tone—
(the Spirit of God hovering over it)
the first harmonic above it:
a major third—slipping into a minor third
God called:
and the universe responded—
with light and music.
From the beginning of space
there has been music
(Bell Labs first heard it in the 1950s...)
Mediæval and Renaissance cosmologists
wrote of it:
there is a music of the spheres!

From the beginning of time
There has been music (*Kyrie! Gloria!*)
Calling from that first *glissando*
gathering from all the forming overtones
Fifth Fourth Octave Third (God be with us!)
Black holes, galaxies, gamma ray bursts, planetary systems—
all have their tones, harmonics, rhythms—
B-flat, D-flat, champagne corks popping—
The future present from the beginning
Gathering from the past.
Athanasius Kircher in the seventeenth century
portrayed the universe
as a magnificent World Organ,
whose six stops were
the six days of Creation.
"Thus," he wrote,
"thus God's wisdom
plays in the sphere
of the worlds."
And Time,
Time
is length of the pipe that is sounding
beneath everything in the universe
Time.
Gathering from the past
The future present in the rising overtones
Called
Gathered.

II. Enlightened: "In the Beginning—Music, Word, Story"

In the beginning
Bereshit bara Elohim
"In the beginning;"
chanted the people of Israel
after exile in Babylon
chanting of voices
singing of the creation of all things
chanting in harmony with the universe's music
"In the beginning, *God*"
they chanted.
Singing of the Beginning
singing of Egypt
singing of the wilderness wandering
To remember—
Music and Word
Having been exiled from Jerusalem
between destroyed Temple past
and future Temple not yet
Wondering if God was indeed still present
in their midst
The people heard the minute details
of the tabernacle in the desert
what God had commanded
to be built to be sewn to be carved to be cast
in exile they could create in their minds
that place that tabernacle
where God had promised
to be present in their midst
creating a Temple of the mind—
through Story and Song and Word
(the Spirit of God hovering over Story)
until the future clothed in the past
would create another Temple in Jerusalem

"God is always on the move
to a new creation,"
writes Terence Fretheim.
"The sanctuary is a world
where God's order prevails."
Tapping into the innate music
of Creation
in chant and psalm and hymn
we too remember
we too clothe the future in the past
we recall
the cosmic story of the merciful God
we sing of Christ's loving sacrifice then
for the future
our future
the creation's future
"In the Beginning was the Word...
and the Word tabernacled among us...
tabernacled among us...
full of grace and truth."

III. Sanctified: "Holy Holy Holy—Here I Will Meet You"

In the tabernacle
In the desert
God commanded
that a mercy seat of pure gold
be crafted above the ark
that housed the covenant—
Bezalel and other craftspeople
were given the skill and knowledge
and the Spirit of God
to make all that God had commanded—
Two cherubim would face each other
wings upraised
overshadowing the ark.
"There," said God,
"There I will meet you."
Holy, Holy, Holy
The *Sanctus* is said to be
the song the cherubim and seraphim
continually sing
before God's throne.
When at dawn
the angel had to leave off
from wrestling with Jacob,
the midrash says,
it was because it was the angel's shift
to sing the *Sanctus* before God.

Song and music can evoke the Holy
Song and music can soften the Heart
so that we remember and hear at last
the story of God,
of God's love,
of God's intent for Creation
There I will meet you...
Martin Luther wrote:
"For the preaching of the Gospel
is nothing less than Christ coming to us,
or our being brought
to him."
Carl Jung said that at the Sanctus
"a window opens to eternity."
There I will meet you...
Alexander Schmemann wrote:
"At the Kiss of Peace
Christ is revealed in our midst
and the assembly enters the *eschaton*."
There I will meet you.
(The Spirit hovering over the assembly...)
There I will meet you

IV. Sustained: "Called to the Future, Which Is Christ"

"There God's eternal wisdom
plays in the sphere of the worlds . . . "
From the primal *glissando* and pedal tone
of the creation of the universe
to the liturgical chanting of the creation story
by the Jewish exiles
to the singing of the *Sanctus*
in the liturgy
the Spirit hovers over
the sacred gift of music
calling us, gathering us,
enlightening, sanctifying,
sustaining.
We call the past into the present
by our song
We remember the future
into which we are called
to rise.
Paul Evdokimov
comments on the traditional Orthodox icon
of the Harrowing of Hell:
"Christ went into Hades saying:
'Come to me, my image and likeness.'"

Augustine wrote in one sermon:
"if you therefore are Christ's body
and members, it is your own mystery
that is placed on the table.
It is your own mystery
that you are receiving."
We are to rise into the image of Christ
The future into which we are called is Christ
The future toward which God's sacred Song
is calling us, is Christ
Christ, the perfect harmony of matter and spirit
Christ, the perfect concord of human and divine
As Irenaeus of Lyons wrote:
"Christ, in immeasurable love,
became what we are
in order to make us what Christ is."
There, God sings,
there I will meet you.

Closing Prayer

O God beyond all thought,
God beyond all sense,
from the beginning
when you sang forth the world,
the Spirit hovered,
and the morning stars sang out alleluia;
when all creation was set in motion
you sang "Beautiful!",
and all the blessed creatures sang out alleluia;
when you met the people Israel
in the wilderness,
the golden cherubim chanted to one another alleluia;
when Jesus the Anointed One,
perfect harmony of human and divine,
entered human flesh
through the open love of Mary his Mother,
the angels sang into the blue night alleluia;
And now here we lift up our hearts
singing together alleluia;
may we meet you in the Song,
may we encounter you in the Word,
may we see you in the Story,
and so met, so encountered, so seen
may you so fill our moments
that every precious breath,
every precious heartbeat,
sings
alleluia.
Amen

THE SPIRIT OF TRANSFORMATION

I. Echoing Down

The Holy Spirit
often gets little attention
in the workings of the church.
Just look at the Apostles' Creed:
God the Father
receives two lines
of profession;
Jesus Christ—
ten lines;
and the Holy Spirit?
One.
True, most of the disputes
in the early church
had to do
with Who Is Jesus Christ?,
but the single line for the Spirit
is rather telling.
But if we look at the life
of the Christian
in the world,
the Holy Spirit
truly deserves more
than one line.
For it is the Holy Spirit
who calls us to faith,
who stirs within us,
deepening our call.

The word catechism
comes from the Greek words
kata = down
and *ekhes* = sound—
so a catechism helps
the teachings of the Spirit
"echo down"
deeply into us
body and soul and mind
echoing down, ringing in us
becoming a part of who we are
echoing down
pressuring us into who we are becoming
echoing down into us.
The sighs of the Holy Spirit
calling, calling
calling us
to trust—to love—to be courageous
calling us
to come home from exile.

II. God Looks on the Heart

Interesting,
when we look at the Bible
to see whom God calls
whom Jesus calls—
how often God calls
and anoints
an unexpected choice
how often God chooses
not only what seems ordinary,
but what seems to be outright flawed,
how often God calls an ordinary person
for a special purpose.
God called to Moses
from a bush aflame
Four times God called
Four times Moses made excuses
saying he wasn't good enough,
gifted enough.
God called
and finally Moses
led a people to freedom.
Nathan the prophet
was instructed by God
to find and anoint a new king
for Israel.
After seeing the eldest seven sons of Jesse
Nathan said,
Isn't there one more?
Nathan asked to see the youngest
who was out in the fields
keeping the sheep
and so anointed
David to be king.

God sent an angel
to an ordinary young woman
to call her to a special purpose:
to bear the Incarnate Word
into the world.
God called Mary,
who gave her consent
and Jesus the Christ
was born as a human person.
Jesus called to ordinary fishermen,
tax collectors,
women,
and a spiritual awakening caught fire.
Who are we?
Who are we—
we say—
that God should call us?
And God answers us,
as God answered the prophet Nathan:
"God does not see as people see—
God looks on the heart."

III. Praying with Our Legs

A rabbinic story:

A rabbi entered a room where his son was praying. The baby was crying in the crib. "Son, can't you hear that there is a baby crying in this room?" "I'm sorry, Father, but I was praying, and I was lost in God." The rabbi replied: "Son, one who is lost in God can see the very fly crawling on the wall."

Prayer is not about
escape from the world—
we are advised to pray
with one eye open—
to see! to see!
to be aware.
Theologian Joseph Sittler
called prayer
the Ultimate Conversation.
Prayer drives us
naked and vulnerable
into an encounter
with both the holy
and the world
where we encounter
not only God
but our own true Self.

Prayer is not just silence
not just words
not just mantras
not just centering
It is all of these and more
It is a letting go
a falling into
the steadfast love
of God.
It is action
It is doing
It is life.
Frederick Douglass,
escaped slave, writer,
and statesman wrote:
"I prayed for twenty years,
but received no answer
until I prayed
with my legs."

IV. *Ubi caritas et amor*

Where charity and love are
there God is.
The Holy Spirit calls us
speaks to us through prayer
gathers us into community
Everything that exists
comes together by community
protons and electrons and neutrons
quarks and muons and bosons
galaxy and black hole and nova
male and female
hydrogen and oxygen
seed and soil and water and sun
Relationship
is the basis of all that is.
the Holy Trinity
models this for us:
Lover, Beloved, Love
Fire, Light, Warmth
Ocean, River, Rain
Father, Son, Spirit.
"It is not good that the human
should be alone,"
said God on the sixth day.
We are made for relationship
We are made for community

In Barbara Kingsolver's novel *The Bean Trees*
the refugee Estevan
tells a story of heaven and hell:
In hell there is a big table
near a hot kettle
of wonderfully fragrant soup.
It smells so delicious.
But everyone there is unhappy.
Everyone is starving—
because the handles of their spoons
are as long as mop handles,
and they can't bring
the delicious soup
up to their mouths.
But heaven—
same table, same pot of soup, same long spoons—
but here everyone is happy
everyone is well-fed
What is different?
they have learned to feed
each other.

V. Growing into Compassion

"God is love,
and whoever abides in love
abides in God
and God abides in them."
There is in our magnificent brain
a segment called
the anterior cingulate cortex
(we need to add to Psalm 148:
"Anterior cingulate cortex,
praise the Lord!")
and here there are special neurons
called von Economo,
or spindle, neurons
They are where empathy
resides in the brain
(Von Economo neurons,
praise the Lord!)
And when we pray to, sing to,
meditate on, contemplate
a loving compassionate God
the number of spindle neurons
in our brain increases
We become more empathetic
more compassionate people
(God is love,
and whoever abides in love
abides in God
and God abides in them…)

And when we do compassionate acts,
when we do loving deeds
the number of spindle neurons
in our brain increases—
we become more empathetic
more compassionate
What kind of God did Jesus embody?
What did Jesus teach us about God?
What do our prayers say about God?
What do our hymns sing about God?
Who are we becoming
in our praying and our singing?
In one of his Easter sermons,
Augustine wrote:
"What is the glory of God?
The glory of God is the one who sings about it.
Become yourselves
the glory you sing of."
(God is love and whoever abides in love abides in God...)

VI. Our Proper Stance

Traditional Orthodox Christian icons
are windows into eternity,
windows into heaven.
In representing events
in the life of Christ
in the life of Mary
of the saints
they help us
"remember the future."
In the traditional icon
of Jesus
washing the feet
of the disciples
all the disciples are the same size
there is no perspective
drifting off into a
vanishing point
at the horizon
in this way
the iconographer
invites us too
into the gathering
into the icon

As we gaze into the upper room
from the fourth wall
we become a part
of this act
of footwashing
of sharing
of humility
of relationship
of community
ubi caritas et amor
Where charity and love are,
there God is.
Jesus here shows us
that our proper stance
toward each other
toward all that God loves
toward creation
is to be kneeling
to be kneeling
with basin
and with
towel.

VII. Becoming the Vine

The Holy Spirit
calls us
into a deepening life
echoing down
into the depths of being.
The Spirit calls us
ordinary people
to do extraordinary things
with its gifts
The Spirit calls us
into a living prayer
connected to God
in all things
The Spirit calls us
into community
into relationship
into compassion
with those bright spindle neurons
firing sparks
of lovingkindness
becoming the glory
we sing of
The Spirit calls us
to live out our lives
connected to Christ the Vine
growing up into sunlight
healthy and rooted
and full of holy,
precious life.
Each of us
holy and precious branches
are connected not only to Christ,

but to each other.
And because we are a part
of the Vine
connected to the Vine
we are in essence
Vine
becoming Christ
becoming love
becoming wounded servants
through all the seasons
of this blessed
blessed life.

Prayer

Holy Spirit,
luminous life,
you echo down
into our deepest, truest selves, calling, gathering,
enlightening,
making all holy.
Dwell here in our midst
setting our hearts on fire
with your love,
that our songs may be true,
our prayers may be noble,
and our lives may be service
kindled by your love,
for you are One with the Father
and the Son
unto all ages of ages.
Amen

QUOTES

Te Deum Laudamus: Let Us Praise God

3 Gregory of Nyssa, *Treatise on the Inscriptions of the Psalms,* fourth century.

3 Martin Franzmann, *Ha! Ha! Among the Trumpets: Sermons by Martin H. Franzmann,* (St. Louis, Concordia Publishing House, 1994), 92.

4 Adam Scotus, "*De triplici genere contemplationis,*" in Patrologia Latina, Vol. 198, Col. 802.

5 Ephrem the Syrian, *Hymns on Paradise,* (Crestwood, New York, St. Vladimir's Press, 1990), XI, 6, 156.

6 Augustine of Hippo, *Sermon 34 on Psalm 149.*

6 Nadia Boulanger, quoted in Don G. Campbell , *Master Teacher: Nadia Boulanger,* (Portland, Pastoral Press, 1982), 95.

7 Paul Westermeyer, *Hymnal Companion to Evangelical Lutheran Worship,* (Minneapolis, Augsburg Fortress, 2010), xxiii.

Worship in Song: Joy, Hope, Peace

12 *The Songs Are Free: Bernice Johnson Reagon and African-American Music,* directed by Gail Pellett, (Public Affairs Television, 1991).

Time, God's Holy Creature

27 Aidan Kavanaugh, *The Elements of Rite: A Handbook of Litugical Style,* (Collegeville, MN, Pueblo, 1982), 27.

33 Rabbi Rami Shapiro, paraphrase and trope on Rabbi Tarfon in *Wisdom of the Jewish Sages: A Modern Reading of Pirke Avot,* (New York, Harmony/Bell Tower (Crown/Random House), 1993), 41.

34 Karl Rahner, as quoted in Judy Cannato, *Field of Compassion,* (Notre Dame, IN, Sorin Books, 2010), ix.

38 Carl Gustav Jung, "VI. The Consecration" in "Transformation Symbolism in the Mass", in Psyche and Symbol (Princeton, Princeton University Press, 1991), 170.

40 Gertrud Mueller Nelson, as shared in an email to the author, November 22, 2005.

The Year in Faith: A Children's Choir Festival

46 John 8:12

Heaven and Earth in Little Space

64 Ephrem the Syrian, *On Faith,* 31:2.

64 Irenaeus, *Adversus haereses,* V, Preface.

66 Psalm 62:11

69 Ursula Le Guin, *A Wizard of Earthsea,* (New York, Houghton Mifflin Harcourt, 1968), ebook edition, Ch. 4.

Beyond All Thought and Fantasy

74 Ephesians 3:18-19

77 Irenaeus, *Adversus Haereses,* V, Preface.

78 Thomas Berry, *The Dream of the Earth,* (San Francisco, Sierra Club, 1988), 106.

83 Abel Herzberg, *Brieven aan mijn Kleinzoon* [*Letters to My Grandson*], (Amsterdam, Querido, 1985), 126. Translated by Nancy Forest, used in Jim Forest, *The Road to Emmaus,* (Maryknoll, NY, Orbis Books, 2007), 144.

84 Jim Forest, "Sister Mary Evelyn Jegen: On Benevolent Glancing," Jim and Nancy Forest, http://jimandnancyforest.com/2014/07/benevolent-glancing/, 2014.

87 Dorothy L. Sayers, *The Devil to Pay,* (Eugene, OR, Wipf and Stock Publishers, 1939), 54.

Jesus Christ, Yesterday, Today, Forever

89 Colossians 1:15-20

90 Richard Rohr, as quoted in "The Living School: Theme 2," Center for Action and Contemplation, https://cac.org/living-school/program-details/lineage-and-themes/. Explored in depth in: Rohr, *Yes, and...:Daily Meditations,* (Cincinnati, Franciscan Media, 2013).

92 Pierre Teilhard de Chardin, "A Sketch of a Personalistic Universe", in *Human Energy,* (New York, Harcourt, 1972). page

94 Isaiah 6:2–3

94 Francisco de Holanda, *De Aetatibus Mundi Imagines.*

95 Pierre Teilhard de Chardin, *The Divine Milieu,* (New York, Harper & Row, 1950), 112.

98 John 12:24

100 John 14:12

Journeys

104 Acts 17:28

108 Poster: "Slave sale notice, To be sold and let by public auction on Monday the 18th of May, 1829.'" Schomburg Center for Research in Black Culture, Manuscripts, Archives and Rare Books Division, The New York Public Library. New York Public Library Digital Collections. Viewed by the author at the National Civil Rights Museum in Memphis, TN.

111 Atttributed to The Kotzker Rebbe, Rabbi Menachem Mendel of Kotzk.

117 John 12:24

Rise, Heart

119 George Herbert, "Easter,"1633.

124 Charles Péguy, *Basic Verities:Prose and Poetry,* translated by Anne and Julian Green, (New York, Pantheon, 1943).

126 George Herbert, "Easter,"1633.

129 Martin Buber, *Tales of the Hasidim, Vol. I,* (New York, Schocken Books, 1991), 251.

130 Augustine, "The New Chant", Sermon 34 on Psalm 149

Praise and Thanksgiving

137 Abraham Joshua Heschel, *No Religion Is an Island,* (Eugene, OR, Wipf and Stock Publishers, 2008), 264.

138 John 15:5

Where Charity and Love Prevail

155 Anthony de Mello, "Who Am I?" from *The Song of the Bird,* (New York, Doubleday, 1982), 99-100.

157 John 15:5

158 Pierre Teilhard de Chardin, *The Divine Milieu,* (New York, Harper & Row, 1950).

We Believe in the Holy Spirit

166 Karl Rahner, as quoted in Judy Cannato, *Field of Compassion,*(Notre Dame, IN, Sorin Books, 2010), ix.

168 Abraham Heschel, *The Prophets,* (New York, HarperCollins, 2001), 9.

169 Abraham Heschel, *The Prophets,* (New York, HarperCollins, 2001), 16.

170 Hildegard von Bingen, *Scivias,* Vision 14.

172 Chinua Achebe, quoted in Hillel Italie and Jon Gambrell, "A Literary Titan, Voice of Africa: Chinua Achebe 1930-2013" in *The Star Tribune,* March 22, 2013.

That We May Be One

184 Anthony de Mello, *One Minute Wisdom,* (New York, Doubleday Image Books, 1988), 150.

192 Pierre Teilhard de Chardin, *The Divine Milieu,* (New York, Harper & Row, 1950), 127.

Songs of the Spirit

196 Everett Fox, *The Schocken Bible, Volume I: The Five Books of Moses,* Genesis 1:1–2, (New York, Schocken Books, 1997).

198 Pierre Teilhard de Chardin, "A Sketch of a Personalistic Universe", in *Human Energy,* (New York, Harcourt, 1972).

199 Pierre Teilhard de Chardin, *The Divine Milieu,* (New York, Harper & Row, 1950), 66.

204 Etty Hillesum, *Etty: The Letters and Diaries of Etty Hillesum, 1941-1943, Complete and Unabridged,* edited by Klaas A. D. Smelik, translated by Arnold J. Pomeranz (Grand Rapids, MI, Eerdmans Publishers, 2002), 307.

206 Dennis Overbye, "Don't Let Them Tell You You're Not at the Center of the Universe", *The New York Times,* April 1, 2016.

207 Karl Rahner, as quoted in Judy Cannato, *Field of Compassion,*(Notre Dame, IN, Sorin Books, 2010), ix.

The Church Reforming

214 Isaiah 43:19

216 Philippians 2:5-7

216 Samuel Torvend, *Luther and the Hungry Poor: Gathered Fragments,* (Minneapolis, Augsburg Fortress, 2008), 10.

218 Revelation 21:5

220 Lamentations 3:22-23

Sing the New Song

224 *The Songs Are Free: Bernice Johnson Reagon and African-American Music*, directed by Gail Pellett, (Public Affairs Television, 1991).

226 Isaiah 40:28

228 Joan Chittister, *Aspects of the Heart*, (New London, CT, Twenty-Third Publications, 2012), 18.

229 Makarios, *Homilies* 43:7.

230 Loren Eiseley, "The Hidden Teacher", in *The Star Thrower* (New York, Harcourt, 1978), 118.

230 Gabriele Uhlein, *Meditations with Hildegard of Bingen*, (Rochester, VT, Bear & Company, 1983), 106.

232 *The Songs Are Free: Bernice Johnson Reagon and African-American Music*, directed by Gail Pellett, (Public Affairs Television, 1991).

Through the Church the Song Goes On

249 Prayer for the Vigil of Pentecost, *Evangelical Lutheran Worship*, (Minneapolis, Augsburg Fortress, 2006), 36.

Holy Spirit, Luminous Life

252 Everett Fox, *The Schocken Bible, Volume I: The Five Books of Moses*, Genesis 1:1–2, (New York, Schocken Books, 1997).

252 Hildegard von Binen, Scivias, Part II, Vision 2.

252 Richard Rohr, "God's First Idea," Center for Action and Contemplation, https://cac.org/gods-first-idea-2019-02-17/. Adapted from Rohr, *The Cosmic Christ*, disc 2 (Center for Action and Contemplation, 2009), and *Eager to Love: The Alternative Way of Francis of Assisi*, (Franciscan Media, 2014).

258 Ursula Le Guin, *A Wizard of Earthsea*, (New York, Houghton Mifflin Harcourt, 1968), ebook edition, Ch. 3.

264 Charles Baudelaire, "Intimate Associations", in *News of the Universe*, edited and translated by Robert Bly, (San Francisco, Sierra Club Books,1980), 44.

264 *Journey of the Universe: An Epic Story of Cosmic, Earth and Human Transformation*, Brian Swimme, directed by David Kennard and Patsy Northcutt, DVD, 2013.

264 Joseph Sittler, "Called to Unity," *The Ecumenical Review*, Vol. 14 (January 1962), 183.

267 Hildegard von Bingen, *De Spiritu Sancto.*

To God I Give My Melody

269 Martin Luther, "Confession Concerning Christ's Supper, "1528.

274 Michael Praetorius, *Syntagma Musicum, I: Musicae Artis Analecta*, 1614.

275 Martin Luther, *"Gelobet seist du, Jesu Christ,"* 1524.

276 Martin Luther, "*Exposition on Psalm 101*," 1534.

277 Martin Luther, *"Vom Himmel hoch, da komm ich her,"* 1535.

278 Michael Praetorius, *Syntagma Musicum, I: Musicae Artis Analecta*, 1614.

279 Martin Luther, 1517 *Exposition of Penitential Psalms*, WA 14

279 Martin Luther, Letter to Spalatin, *Lutheran Worship*, 49:3

279 Martin Luther, *"Mit Fried und Freud ich fahr dahin,"* 1524.

To God I Give My Melody, cont.

280 Martin Luther, *"Christ lag in Todesbanden,"* 1524.

280 *"Victimae Paschali laudes,"* sequence for Easter, eleventh century.

281 Martin Luther, *"Christ lag in Todesbanden,"* 1524.

282 Martin Luther, Preface to Georg Rhau's *Symphoniae iucundae,* 1538.

283 Martin Luther, *"A Preface for All Good Hymnals,"* 1538.

283 Martin Luther, *"Komm Gott Schöpfer Heiliger Geist,"* 1524.

285 Martin Luther, *"Mitten wir im Leben sind,"* 1524.

Rise, Remember Well the Future

287 Martin Luther, *The Small Catechism,* The Apostles' Creed, Third Article, 1529.

288 Gregory of Nyssa, *Treatise on the Inscriptions of the Psalms,* fourth century.

291 Terence E. Fretheim, *Interpretation: A Bible Commentary for Teaching and Preaching Exodus,* (Louisville, KY, Westminster John Knox Press, 2010), 271.

291 John 1:1

292 Exodus 25:22

293 Carl Gustav Jung, "VI. The Consecration" in "Transformation Symbolism in the Mass", in *Psyche and Symbol* (Princeton, Princeton University Press, 1991), 170.

293 Alexander Schmemann, *For the Life of the World* (Crestwood, NY, St. Vladimir's Press, 1973), 37.

294 Athanasius Kircher, *Musurgia universalis,* 1650.

294 Vigen Guroian, *The Melody of Faith: Theology in an Orthodox Key,* (Grand Rapids, MI, Wm. B. Eerdmans Publicing Co., 2010), 134.

295 Augustine of Hippo, Sermon 272, "On the Nature of the Sacrament of the Eucharist."

295 Irenaeus, *Adversus Haereses,* Book 5, Preface.

The Spirit of Transformation

301 Samuel 16:7

303 Frederick Douglass, quoted in Joan Chittister, *The Breath of the Soul: Reflections On Prayer* (New London, CT: Twenty-Third Publications, 2010), 23.

306 1 John 4:16

307 Augustine of Hippo, "The New Chant", Sermon 34 on Psalm 149

308 Gregory of Nyssa, *Treatise on the Inscriptions of the Psalms,* fourth century.

APPENDIX I

HYMN FESTIVAL STRUCTURE
A BASIC FORM FOR A FESTIVAL OF HYMNS

Opening Hymn

Invocation

Prayer

[Possible Scripture Reading

Reading or Meditation

Hymn or Anthem or both]

*(This sequence may be repeated for a central core of perhaps three to seven hymns or choral works or combinations of the two.)**

Closing Prayers

Closing Hymn

Benediction

OR

Benediction

Closing Hymn

There is much room for flexibility and creativity within this form: it can be simple or festive. Hymns may be varied as to instrumentation, and the stanzas may be assigned various segments of the congregation (children, choir, sopranos and altos, tenors and basses, left side, right side (generally as the mood of the text suggests. Unaccompanied stanzas and stanzas in harmony can well establish the congregated people as a unified voice, and truly form "a body for praise."

*A hymn festival with opening and closing hymns, and a core of seven hymns or anthems with reflections will create a service of about one hour and twenty minutes.

APPENDIX II

THE HYMN FESTIVALS

In the hymn festival and choral festival outlines that follow, the hymns listed were those in the original design of the festival, but they can be taken, for the most part, as suggestions, unless the hymns are quoted in the reflections, as in *To God I Give My Melody*. Anyone who chooses to use these hymn festivals as a template can surely adapt and choose carefully from the great body of hymnody for a particular occasion or gathering. In cases where hymns were used that I have written and that are not in any major hymnal, the hymn name is followed by an asterisk and note of which volume of collected hymns it can be found in; at the time of this writing there are three volumes published by Augsburg Fortress.

Composer's last names follow anthems in parantheses. A full listing of choral publications begins on page 332.

***Te Deum Laudamus*: Let Us Praise God**

Opening Hymn:	Holy God, We Praise Your Name
Invocation	
Reading:	Colossians 3:12-17
Chant:	*Te Deum* (sung by all)
Reflection I:	Theology and Song
Hymn:	As newborn stars were stirred to song
Hymn:	Oh, Sing to God Above
Reflection II:	The Word and Song
Hymn:	Christ Jesus Lay In Death's Strong Bands
Hymn:	I Want Jesus to Walk with Me
Reflection III:	Community and Song
Hymn:	O Living Breath of God
Hymn:	If You But Trust in God to Guide You
Closing Prayer	
Hymn:	Lord, Thee I Love with All My Heart

Worship in Song: Joy, Hope, Peace

Prelude: *Salvation Is Created* (Chesnokov)
The Word Was God (Powell)
Witness (Hogan)
Have Ye Not Known?/Ye Shall Have A Song (Thompson)
Reflection I: Joy
Hymn: Joyful, Joyful, We Adore Thee
Anthem: *Zikr* and/or *Ute Sundance* (Sperry)
Prayer (Joy)
Reflection II: Hope
Anthem: *I Lift Up My Eyes* (D. Cherwien)
Prayer (Hope)
Reflection III: Peace
Anthem: *There We Shall Rest* (Arnesen)
Prayer (Peace)
Hymn: Come By Here (Brown)
Closing Prayer
Closing Benediction: *The Lord Bless You and Keep You* (Lutkin)

A Thousand Voices Sing Praise

Kyrie: "The Spheres" from *Sunrise Mass* (Gjeilo)
Opening Hymn: All Creatures of Our God and King
Invocation
Reflection I: Even the Sun Has a Song
Hymn: Angels We Have Heard on High
Anthem: *Lord Now Lettest Thou* (Rachmaninoff)
Reflection II: Songs of Our Ancestors
Hymn: God Who Stretched the Spangled Heavens
Reflection III: Letting Go
Anthem: *Psalm 2,* Op. 78 (Mendelssohn)
Reading: 2 Corinthians 5:6-10, 14-17
Hymn: Love Divine, All Loves Excelling
Reading: Mark 4:26-34
Anthem: *Keep Your Hand on the Plow* (Jennings)
Reflection IV: Songs of Peace
Anthem: *Agnus Dei: Phoenix* (Gjeilo)
Anthem: *Dona nobis pacem* (Bach)
Prayers
Hymn: To You Before the Close of Day
Benediction

Time, God's Holy Creature

Opening Hymn:	All People That on Earth Do Dwell
Reflection I:	Word
Hymn:	The Word of God Is Source and Seed
Reflection II:	Story
Hymn:	O Love, How Deep, How Broad, How High
Reflection III:	Halakhah
Hymn:	What Does the Lord Require
Reflection IV:	Wisdom
Hymn:	Come to Us, Creative Spirit
Reflection V:	Sabbath
Hymn:	What Is This Place
Reflection VI:	Eucharist
Hymn:	When Twilight Comes
Reflection VII:	Procession of Saints
Hymn:	Great God, Whose Story Age to Age* (Cherwien, III)
Closing Prayers	
Benediction	
Closing Hymn:	O God Our Help in Ages Past

The Year In Faith: A Children's Choir Festival

Opening Anthem:	*Let the Whole Creation Cry* (Kosche)
Reflection I:	Let the Whole Creation Cry
Anthem:	*Lord of the Dance* (Pilkington)
Reflection II:	Advent
Anthem:	*The World's True Light* (Page)
Reflection III:	Christmas
Anthem:	*Angels' Carol* (Rutter)
Reflection IV:	Lent
Anthem:	*A Lenten Love Song* (Kemp)
Reflection V:	Holy Week
Anthem:	*Hosanna! Blessed Is He That Comes* (Gregor/Bitgood)
Reflection VI:	Easter
Anthem:	*All Shall Be Well* (Larsen)
Reflection VII:	The Second Part of the Story
Anthem:	*Christ Alone* (Beckstrand)
Reflection VIII:	The Circle of the Seasons
Anthem:	*A Time To Sing Praise* (Leaf)

Heaven and Earth in Little Space

Opening Hymn:	O Morning Star, How Fair and Bright!
Invocation	
Reflection I:	Heaven/Earth
Hymn:	A Stable Lamp Is Lighted
Reflection II:	Power/Vulnerability
Hymn:	Weary of All Trumpeting
Reflection III:	Eternity/Time
Hymn:	How Small Our Span of Life
Reflection IV:	Divine/Human
Hymn:	Peace Came to Earth
Reflection V:	Past/Future
Hymn:	Crown Him with Many Crowns
Reflection VI:	Sovereign/Servant
Hymn:	You Have Come Down to the Lakeshore
Reflection:	Alpha/Omega
Hymn:	Of the Father's Love Begotten
Prayer	
Benediction	
Closing Hymn:	Christus Paradox

Beyond All Thought and Fantasy

Opening Hymn:	O Love, How Deep, How Broad, How High
Reflection I:	Beyond All Thought and Fantasy
Hymn:	All My Hope on God Is Founded
Reflection II:	That God Should Take Our Mortal Form
Hymn:	Once in Royal David's City
Reflection III:	For Us
Hymn:	*Ubi caritas et amor*
Reflection IV:	For Us Baptized
Hymn:	I Bind Unto Myself Today
Reflection V:	For Us He Prayed, For Us He Taught
Hymn:	Take My Life and Let It Be
Reflection VI:	By Words and Signs
Hymn:	There Is a Balm in Gilead
Reflection VII:	Still Seeking Not Himself, but Us
Hymn:	When Twilight Comes
Prayer	
Benediction	
Closing Hymn:	Now Rest Beneath Night's Shadow

Jesus Christ, Yesterday, Today, and Forever

Opening chant: Jesus Christ, Yesterday, Today, and Forever
Anthem: *O vis aeternitatis* (Hildegard von Bingen)
alternating with: *Corde Natus*/Of the Father's Love Begotten
Hymn: As Newborn Stars Were Stirred to Song
Reading: Colossians 1:15–20

Kyrie

Anthem: "The Spheres" from *Sunrise Mass* (Gjeilo)
Reflection I: Image of the Invisible God - *Kyrie* (Advent)
Hymn: Creator of the Stars of Night

Gloria

Anthem: "Gloria" from *Missa Criolla* (Ramirez)
Reflection II: Firstborn of Creation - *Gloria* (Christmas)
Hymn: Peace Came to Earth

Sanctus

Anthem: *Sanctus* (Widor)
Reflection III: In Him All Things in Heaven and on Earth Were Created - *Sanctus* (Epiphany, Baptism, or Transfiguration)
Hymn: O Morning Star, How Fair and Bright!

Benedictus

Anthem: "Benedictus" from *Messe* (Martin)
Reflection IV: In Him All Things Hold Together - *Benedictus* (Entry Into Jerusalem)
Hymn: Give Me Jesus
Chant: Jesus Christ, Yesterday, Today, and Forever (Toolan)

Agnus dei

Anthem: *Lamb of God* (Christiansen)
Reflection V: He Is the Beginning, the Firstborn of the Dead - *Agnus dei* (Good Friday/Easter)
Hymn: There in God's Garden
Hymn: Christ Is Arisen, Alleluia

Dona nobis pacem

Reflection VI.: For in Him All the Fullness of God Was Pleased to Dwell - *Dona nobis pacem* (Ascension or Christ the King)
Anthem: *Nada Te Turbe* (Runestad)

Nunc dimittis

Closing prayer
Anthem: *Nunc dimittis* (Arkhangelsky)

Journeys

Opening Hymn:	God of Grace and God of Glory
Invocation	
Reflection I:	Journey in God
Hymn:	O Heart of God, O Chamber of the Holy* (Cherwien, III)
Reflection II:	Journey with Purpose
Hymn:	O God, O Lord of Heaven and Earth
Reflection III:	Journey with Christ
Hymn:	I Want Jesus to Walk with Me
Reflection IV:	Journey through Wilderness
Hymn:	Through the Night of Dark and Sorrow
Reflection V:	Journey as Community
Hymn:	Blest Be the Tie That Binds
Reflection VI:	Journey to Christ-likeness
Hymn:	He Is the Way
Reflection VII:	Journey in the Spirit
Hymns in alternation:	Now to the Holy Spirit Let Us Pray
	Creator Spirit, Heavenly Dove (*Veni creator Spiritus*)
Prayer	
Benediction	
Closing Hymn:	The Day You Gave Us, Lord, Has Ended

Rise, Heart

Opening Hymn:	Christ Is Arisen, Alleluia!
Invocation	
Reflection I:	Rise heart; thy Lord is risen
Hymn:	There In God's Garden
Reflection II:	Who takes thee by the hand
Hymn:	Lord Jesus, You Shall Be My Song (*Les Petits Soeurs*)
Reflection III:	That thou likewise with him mayst rise
Hymn:	Day of Arising
Reflection IV:	That, as his death calcined thee to dust
Hymn:	Joyful Is the Dark
Reflection V:	His Life may make thee gold
Hymn:	How Firm a Foundation
Reflection VI:	And much more, just.
Hymn:	The Church of Christ In Ev'ry Age
Prayer	
Closing Hymn:	When Twilight Comes

Praise and Thanksgiving

Opening Hymn: Now Thank We All Our God
Reflection I: A Galaxy Is an Activity
Hymn: Creator of the Stars of Night
Reflection II: Know Before Whom You Stand
Hymn: The God of Abraham Praise
Reflection III: The Vine and the Branches
Hymn: O Blessed Spring
Reflection IV: Singing Truth
Hymn: If You But Trust in God to Guide You
Reflection V: Who Was This Jesus?
Hymn: Give Me Jesus
Reflection VI : There Is a Rhythm to Life
Hymn: The Day You Gave Us, Lord
Prayer
Benediction
Closing Hymn: Rise, O Church

Where Charity And Love Prevail

Opening Hymn: Voices Raised To You We Offer
Reflection I: Where
Anthem: *Betelehemu*
Hymn: Mothering God, You Gave Me Birth
Anthem: *Mary's Cradle Song* (Nelson)
Reflection II: Charity
Hymn: When the Poor Ones
Anthem: *I Got Shoes* (Shaw/Parker)
Reflection III: And
Hymn: Signs and Wonders
Anthem: *Hold On!* (Garrett)
Reflection IV: Love
Hymn: Creating God, Your Fingers Trace
Reflection V: Are
Hymn: Blest Be the Tie That Binds
Anthem: "Water" from *From Light to Light* (McDermid)
Reflection VI: There
Hymn: Jesus Priceless Treasure
Reflection VII: God
Hymn: God of Many Names
Reflection VIII: Is
Anthem: *Oculus non vidit* (Dubra)
Hymn: O Day of Peace
Prayer
Closing Hymn: Now All the Woods Are Sleeping

We Believe in the Holy Spirit

Opening Hymn: Holy God, We Praise Your Name
Reflection I: We believe in the Holy Spirit...the giver of life...
Hymn: O Spirit of Life, O Spirit of God
Reflection II: ...who has spoken through the prophets
Hymn: O God of Light
Reflection III: We believe in one holy catholic and apostolic church
Hymn: When Twilight Comes
Reflection IV: We acknowledge one baptism for the forgiveness of sins
Hymn: O Blessed Spring
Reflection V: We look for the resurrection of the dead
Hymn: Shall We Gather at the River
Reflection VI: and the life of the world to come
Hymn: O Day of Peace
Reflection VII: Amen
Hymn: Creator of the Stars of Night
Prayers
Benediction
Closing Hymn: God, Who Made the Earth and Heaven

That We May Be One

Opening Hymn: Hail Thee, Festival Day
Reflection I: The Road to Emmaus
Hymn: Day of Arising
Reflection II: Our Hearts Burn within Us
Hymn: Abide with Me
Reflection III: The Good Shepherd
Hymn: The Lord's My Shepherd
Reflection IV: That Thursday Night
Hymn: Rise, O Sun of Righteousness
Reflection V: That They May Be One
Hymn: Lord, Who the Night You Were Betrayed
Reflection VI: The High Priestly Prayer
Hymn: Blest Be the Tie That Binds
Reflection VII: Christ Ascending on High
Hymn: Dear Christians, One and All, Rejoice
Prayers
Benediction
Closing Hymn: Love Divine, All Loves Excelling

Songs of the Spirit

Opening Chant: *Veni creator Spiritus*
Hymn: Come, Holy Spirit, Our Souls Inspire
Reflection I: This-ness
Anthem: *Veni Creator* (Pärt)
Hymn: Praise the Spirit in Creation
Reflection II: Matter and Spirit
Hymn: As the Wind Song
Reflection III: Wildfire
Hymn: O God of Fire, O Word of Flame* (Cherwien, III)
Reflection IV: Rose Petals
Hymn: Like the Murmur of the Dove's Song
Anthem: *Listen Sweet Dove* (G. Ives)
Reflection V: Living in the Spirit
Hymn: Ev'ry Time I Feel the Spirit
Reflection VI: Light Cones
Hymn: Canticle of the Turning
Reflection VII: Spirit-verbs: Becoming
Hymn: Spirit of the Living God
Anthem: *Veni Sancte Spiritus* (Rutter)
Reflection VIII: From Wonder to Peace
Closing Hymn: Come Down, O Love Divine

The Church Reforming

Opening hymn: A Mighty Fortress Is Our God
Reflection I: A New Thing
Hymn: Unexpected and Mysterious
Hymn: From Heaven Above
Hymn: Midnight Stars Make Bright the Skies
Hymn: Christ When For Us You Were Baptized
Reflection II: Stepping Beyond
Hymn: Bless Now, O God, the Journey
Hymn: O Sacred Head, Now Wounded
Hymn: Christ Jesus Lay in Death's Strong Bands
Hymn: Christ Has Arisen, Alleluia!
Hymn: Day of Arising
Reflection III: Becoming a New Creation
Hymn: O Living Breath of God
Hymn: God of Tempest, God of Whirlwind
Reflection IV: New Every Morning
Closing hymn: Holy God, We Praise Your Name

Sing the New Song

Opening Hymn:	Voices Raised to You We Offer
Invocation	
Hymns in alternation:	Praise to the Lord, the Almighty
	Come All You People
Anthem:	*Norwegian Alleluia* (Arnesen)
Reflection I:	Getting to Singing
Hymn:	The Only Son from Heaven
Hymn:	At the Name of Jesus
Reflection II:	Singing Story
Anthem:	*O salutaris hostia* (Ešenvalds)
Hymn:	Blessed Assurance
Reflection III:	Tranforming Love
Setting:	*Create in Me a Clean Heart* (Fryxell)
Hymn:	Crashing Waters At Creation
Hymn:	Children of the Heavenly Father (Berg)
Reflection IV:	Visible Love
Chant:	*Spiritus Sanctus vivificans vita* with
	Veni creator and *Veni Sancte Spiritus*
Hymn:	O Holy Spirit, Root of Life
Anthem:	*Ev'ry Time I Feel the Spirit* (Spiritual)
Reflection V:	The Heart of God
Hymn:	Rise, O Church, Like Christ Arisen
Anthem:	*Lord God, You Have Called Your Servants* (McDermid)

Through the Church the Song Goes On

Opening Hymn:	Voices Raised to You We Offer
Reflection I:	Flight of the Dove
Hymn:	Now to the Holy Spirit Let Us Pray
Reflection II:	Our Ancestor Song
Hymn:	Awake, My Heart, with Gladness
Reflection III:	The Dancing Hymn
Hymn:	In Thee Is Gladness
Reflection IV:	Fortunatus and Neale
Hymn:	Sing, My Tongue, the Glorious Battle
Reflection V:	The Poet's Vision
Hymn:	When Our Song Says Peace
Reflection VI:	Hymns Forming People
Hymn:	O Grant Us, Christ, a Deep Humility* (Cherwien, I)
Reflection VII:	The Spirit Hovers over the World
Hymn:	When Twilight Comes
Prayer	
Closing Hymn:	Holy God, We Praise Your Name

Holy Spirit, Luminous Life

Anthem:	*Holy Spirit, Luminous Life* (Farlee)
Opening hymn:	All Creatures, Worship God Most High
Invocation	
Reflection I:	Holy Spirit, Living and Life-giving
Hymn:	O Living Breath of God
Reflection II:	moving all that lives, you are the root of all creation
Hymn:	Still, I Search for My God
Anthem:	*The Heavens Are Telling* (Haydn)
Reflection III:	You wash all things clean
Anthem:	*Like As the Hart* (Howells)
Hymn:	Come, O Spirit, Come to Us* (tr. Cherwien, III)
Reflection IV:	scrubbing away their mistakes, their guilt
Hymn:	Out of the Depths
Reflection V:	anointing and healing their wounds
Anthem:	"Agnus Dei," from *Requiem* (Rutter)
Hymn:	There Is a Balm in Gilead
Reflection VI:	You are Life, luminous, shining with praise
Hymn:	Light Dawns on a Weary World
Reflection VII:	renewing and reviving all
Hymn:	Gracious Spirit, Hear Our Pleading
Reflection VIII:	The Spirit of Eight
Closing hymn:	I Bind Unto Myself Today

To God I Give My Melody

Opening hymn:	Isaiah in a Vision Did of Old
Invocation	
Reflection I:	Steeped in the Church Fathers
Hymn:	Savior of the Nations, Come
Reflection II:	Classical Latin Poetry
Hymn:	All Praise to You, Eternal Lord
Reflection III:	Aesop and Story
Hymn:	From Heaven Above to Earth I Come
Reflection IV:	A Love of Song
Hymn:	In Peace and Joy I Now Depart
Reflection V:	Singing Theology
Hymns in alternation:	Christians to the Paschal Victim
	Christ Jesus Lay in Death's Strong Bands
Reflection VI:	The Handmaid of God
Hymn:	Creator Spirit, Heavenly Dove
Reflection VII:	Seeking Peace That the World Cannot Give
Hymn:	Even As We Live Each Day
Prayers	
Benediction	
Closing Hymn:	Grant Peace, We Pray in Mercy, Lord

Rise, Remember Well the Future

Called

Opening Chant:	*Veni Sancte Spiritus* (Taizé)
in alternation with:	*Spiritus Sanctus vivificans vita* (Hildegard von Bingen)
Hymn:	Creator of the Stars of Night

Gathered

Invocation	
Reflection I.	Called/Gathered: "In the Beginning—Music"
Anthem:	"Kyrie"from *Missa Papae Marcelli* (Palestrina)
Anthem:	*South African Gloria* (Roberts)

Enlightened

Reflection II.	Enlightened: "In the Beginning—Music, Word, Story"
Chant (choir):	Christians, To the Paschal Victim (*Victimae paschali laudes*)
Hymns in alternation:	Christ Is Arisen (*Christ ist erstanden*)
	Christ Jesus Lay In Death's Strong Bands
Anthem in alternation:	*Also hat Gott die Welt geliebt* (Schütz)

Sanctified

Reflection III.	Sanctified: "Holy Holy Holy—Here I Will Meet You"
Motet:	*Der Geist hilft unser Schwachheit auf* (Bach)
Hymn:	Come To Us, Creative Spirit
Anthem:	*Sanctus/Benedictus,* Op. 36 (Widor)
Hymn:	Spirit of God, Resound In Us* (Cherwien, III)

Sustained

Reflection IV.	Sustained: "Called to the Future, Which Is Christ"
Anthem:	*Guide My Feet* (Graves)
Hymn:	Lord Jesus, You Shall Be My Song (*Les Petits Soeurs)*
Anthem:	*Lord God, You Have Called Your Servants* (McDermid)
Closing prayer:	"The Music of Heaven," in *My God, My Glory* by Eric Milner-White
Benediction	
Closing Hymn:	The Day You Gave Us, Lord, Has Ended

The Spirit of Transformation

Anthem:	*Ubi Caritas et amor* (Duruflé)
Opening Hymn:	Of the Father's Love Begotten
Reflection I:	Echoing Down
Hymn:	Now to the Holy Spirit Let Us Pray
Reflection II:	God Looks on the Heart
Hymn:	You Have Come Down to the Lakeshore
Reflection III:	Praying with Our Legs
Hymn:	Ev'ry Time I Feel the Spirit
Reflection IV:	*Ubi caritas et amor*
Hymn:	Come Now, O Prince of Peace
Reflection V:	Growing into Compassion
Hymn:	Love Divine, All Loves Excelling
Reflection VI:	Our Proper Stance
Hymn:	Blest Be the Tie That Binds
Hymn:	Joyful, Joyful, We Adore Thee
Reflection VII:	Becoming the Vine
Hymn:	O Blessed Spring
Prayer	
Benediction	
Closing Hymn:	A Mighty Fortress Is Our God

APPENDIX III

CHORAL PUBLICATIONS

"Agnus Dei" from *Requiem* (John Rutter)
Oxford University Press (9780193380707)

"Benedictus" from *Messe pour double chœur a capella* (Frank Martin)
Bärenreiter Verlag (BA 7594)

"Gloria" from *Missa Criolla* (Ariel Ramirez)
Alfred Publishing (LG51596)

"Kyrie" from *Missa Papae Marcelli* (G. P. Palestrina)
Kalmus Classic Editions (K06365)

"The Spheres" from *Sunrise Mass* (Ola Gjeilo)
Walton Music (WW1464)

"Water" from *From Light to Light* (J. Aaron McDermid)
MorningStar Music (MSM-70-030)

A Lenten Love Song (Helen Kemp)
Choristers Guild (CGA486)

A Time to Sing Praise (Robert Leaf)
Choristers Guild (CGA615)

Agnus Dei: Phoenix (Ola Gjeilo)
Walton Music (WW1446)

All Shall Be Well (Libby Larsen)
E. C. Schirmer (4261)

Also hat Gott die Welt geliebt (Heinrich Schütz)
Several publishers

Angels' Carol (John Rutter)
Oxford University Press (9780193431263)

Benediction (*The Lord Bless You and Keep You*) (Peter C. Lutkin)
Alfred (00-GCMR02479)

Betelehemu (Babtunde Olatunji and Wendell Whalum, arr. Barrington Brooks)
Lawson-Gould (LG52647)

Christ Alone (William Beckstrand)
MorningStar Music (MSM-50-6107)

Create in Me a Clean Heart (J. G. Winer/adapt. Regina Fryxell)
Service Book and Hymnal, Setting 2, Offertory III

Der Geist hilft unser Schwachheit auf (J. S. Bach)
Several publishers

Dona nobis pacem (J. S. Bach)
Several publishers

Ev'ry Time I Feel the Spirit (Spiritual)
Several publishers

Guide My Feet (Avis D. Graves)
GIA Publications (G-5952)

Hold On! (Marques Garrett)
Walton Music (WW1402)

Holy Spirit, Luminous Life (Robert Buckley Farlee)
Farlee, Unpublished Manuscript

Hosanna! Blessed Is He That Comes (Christian Gregor/Roberta Bitgood)
Alfred (00-GCMR01345)

I Got Shoes (Robert Shaw/Alice Parker)
Alfred (00-LG51116)

I Lift Up My Eyes (David Cherwien)
MorningStar Music (MSM-50-8602)

Keep Your Hand on the Plow (Joseph H. Jennings)
Hinshaw Music (HMC2051)

Lamb of God (F. Melius Christiansen)
Augsburg Fortress (ISBN: 9780800652593)

Like As the Hart (Herbert Howells)
Oxford University Press (ISBN: 9780193501638)

Listen Sweet Dove (Grayston Ives)
Royal School of Church Music (A0042)

Lord God, You Have Called Your Servants (J. Aaron McDermid)
MorningStar Music (MSM-50-8951)

Lord Now Lettest Thou (Sergei Rachmaninoff)
E. C. Schirmer (7825)

Lord of the Dance (Sydney Carter/Steve Pilkington)
Selah (422-815)

Mary's Cradle Song (Ron Nelson)
Beautiful Star Publishing (BSP-251)

Nada Te Turbe (Jake Runestad)
Jake Runestad Music (JR0028)

Norwegian Alleluia (Kim André Arnesen)
Santa Barbara Music Publishing (SBMP1393)

Nunc dimittis (Alexander Arkhangelsky)
Several publishers

O salutaris hostia (Ēriks Ešenvalds)
Musica Baltica (MB0993)

O vis aeternitatis (Hildegard von Bingen)
Several publishers

Oculus non vidit (Rihards Dubra)
Musica Baltica (MB0328)

Psalm 2, Op. 78 (Felix Mendelssohn)
Several publishers

Salvation Is Created (Paul Chesnokov)
Several publishers

Sanctus/Benedictus, Opus 36 (Charles-Marie Widor)
Éditions Alphonse Leduc - Hamelle & Cie (ALHA09240)

South African Gloria (William Bradley Roberts)
MorningStar Music (MSM-50-1215)

Spiritus Sanctus vivificans vita (Hildegard von Bingen)
Several publishers

The Heavens Are Telling (Joseph Haydn)
Several publishers

The Word Was God (Rosephanye Powell)
Gentry Publications (08738700)

The World's True Light (Anna Laura Page)
Augsburg (ISBN: 9780800678395)

There We Shall Rest (Kim André Arnesen)
Santa Barbara Music Publishing (SBMP1371)

Ubi Caritas et amor (Maurice Duruflé)
Several publishers

Veni Creator (Arvo Pärt)
Universal Editions (UE33398)

Veni Sancte Spiritus (John Rutter)
Oxford University Press (ISBN: 9780193504905)

Witness (Moses Hogan)
Hal Leonard (08743357)

Have Ye Not Known?/Ye Shall Have a Song (Randall Thompson)
E. C. Schirmer (1753)

Ute Sundance (Valerie Naranjo/Ethan Sperry)
Earthsongs (S-343)

Zikr (A. R. Rahman/Ethan Sperry)
Earthsongs (S-253)